TEEN LIFE 411™

I'M DEPRESSED.

NOW WHAT?

MICHAEL L. OWENS
AND
AMY GELMAN

ROSEN
PUBLISHING®

New York

Published in 2012 by The Rosen Publishing Group, Inc.
29 East 21st Street, New York, NY 10010

Copyright © 2012 by The Rosen Publishing Group, Inc.

First Edition

Library of Congress Cataloging-in-Publication Data

Owens, Michael, 1978–
I'm depressed, now what? / Michael Owens, Amy Gelman.
   p. cm.—(Teen life 411)
Includes bibliographical references and index.
ISBN 978-1-4488-4656-6 (library binding)
1. Depression, Mental—Juvenile literature. I. Gelman, Amy, 1961–
II. Title.
RC537.O95 2012
616.85'27—dc22

2010044964

Manufactured in the United States of America

CPSIA Compliance Information: Batch #S11YA: For further information, contact Rosen Publishing, New York, New York, at 1-800-237-9932.

CONTENTS

Almost everyone has at one time or another turned to a friend and said, "I'm depressed." Feeling a certain amount of sadness and pain is a part of life. Sometimes people feel depressed because of a specific event, such as a relative dying, a close friend moving away, or breaking up with a boyfriend or girlfriend. At other times, we may feel depressed for no apparent reason. Those times may be more difficult to understand than when we feel sad in response to an event, but even inexplicable sadness is usually normal if it is temporary.

For millions of people in the United States, however, depression is not a passing mood but a serious illness. People with clinical depression, as the disease is generally called, may experience periods of severe sadness, loss of

Nearly everyone experiences depression. Adolescence can be a trying time due to all the changes going on, which makes battling depression all the more difficult.

interest in activities that once gave them pleasure, lack of energy, feelings of guilt and worthlessness, and even thoughts of suicide. Like the everyday "blues" that most people experience, the mental disorder called depression may be situational, which means it is triggered by a difficult or painful event, or it may be chronic, which means it lasts for an extended period of time.

According to the National Institute of Mental Health (NIMH), about 14.8 million adults in the United States have depression. Nearly two million teenagers (ages twelve to eighteen) are affected by this disorder as well. In April 2009, the U.S. Preventive Services Task Force, which sets guidelines for doctors on many health issues, recommended that all American teenagers get screened for depression, as long as there are appropriate screening tests to ensure accurate diagnosis, treatment, and follow-up care. This serious medical illness affects emotions, thoughts, behaviors, and health. People might feel hopeless, deeply unhappy, or unconnected to friends and family members. They lose interest in relationships, school, and social activities.

Depression can continue for several weeks, months, or even longer. The symptoms vary for each person. Common symptoms include feeling negative, sleeping too much or too little, and weight gain or loss. Small tasks, such as making your bed or brushing your teeth, can seem like a huge undertaking. In very serious cases, people may even have thoughts of hurting themselves. Depression can usually be treated successfully, though, and a variety of treatments are available. Treatment for teens usually includes therapy or a combination of anti-depressant medications and therapy.

Depression can affect anyone at any time. Even young children may be diagnosed with depression, although this is not as common as it is in adults and teenagers. According to the NIMH, approximately four of every one hundred teenagers become seriously depressed each year.

Left untreated, depression can worsen, and the depressed person may begin to feel hopeless and lose interest in life. At its worst, depression can lead to sui-cidal thoughts and actions. Fortunately scientists are finding more and more successful treatments for depres-sion each year, ranging from psychological counseling and therapy to medication. Although no surefire, perma-nent cure for depression exists, psychiatrists, researchers, and other experts have learned a great deal about the causes, symptoms, and best treatments for this complex disease, and the outlook for people with depression con-tinues to improve.

Until relatively recently, most experts focused on the psychological causes of depression. Depression can be triggered by any number of psychological events and factors, including abuse or other trauma during child-hood; the loss of an important relationship, such as in a divorce; excessive stress; or a major life change. Researchers now believe, however, that there is also a significant physical component to depression. In recent years, as scientists have learned more about the way the brain functions, they have been able to identify certain chemicals in the brain that affect the way we think and feel. Specifically, some of the chemicals known as neurotransmitters are believed to play an important role in determining whether or not a person will be prone to depression.

DEPRESSION AND ADOLESCENCE

Adolescence is a difficult time for nearly everyone. In addition to the physical changes that puberty brings, adolescence is a time of great emotional change. Many teenagers feel restricted by their parents' rules and look for ways to challenge them. They find themselves caught between childhood and adulthood, with more responsibility than they had in their pre-teen years. Teens may begin dating and dealing with romantic and sexual relationships, with all the emotional ups and downs that those relationships can bring. Friends from childhood may find that they have grown apart, and feelings of loneliness are common. Even for popular, confident teens, though, adolescence can be a tough adjustment.

It is not surprising, then, that many people with depression experience their first serious episode when they are teenagers. This is particularly likely if either or both of a teen's parents have experienced depression. As with an adult, a teen's depression may be brought on by a specific event or series of events, such as conflict with parents or trouble in school, but it is also possible for depression to strike for no apparent

> While most people experience depression at some point in their lives, the teenage years are typically when depression first surfaces.

reason. In addition, the teen years are the time when many people with bipolar disorder first show symptoms, although teens who are bipolar may have more depressive periods than manic ones. About four out of every one hundred teenagers become clinically depressed each year, and this rate is rising. Statistics also show that depressed teenagers are more likely to attempt or commit suicide than depressed adults are. This is why it is especially important for teens who are at risk of committing suicide to seek help.

The Warning Signs

Many—perhaps even most—people go through rocky periods and emotional ups and downs during their teens. It almost seems to be a necessary part of figuring out your own identity as you approach adulthood. Emotions and situations tend to seem more dramatic in adolescence than they did in childhood, and mood swings are common for teenagers. It is also common for teens to argue with or withdraw from their parents. High school is very often a contributing factor to the turmoil of adolescence because the atmosphere at many schools is competitive, cliquish, and high pressure, which can make it hard for teens to maintain strong self-esteem. This can make it difficult for concerned parents, teachers, and family physicians to tell whether a teen who is irritable, withdrawn, self-deprecating, moody, or overemotional is truly depressed or merely going through the normal "growing pains" of adolescence. For that reason, it is helpful to be aware of the signs of clinical depression so that you can recognize it in your friends or yourself.

Depressed teens tend to exhibit behavior that is similar to that of depressed adults, with some additional signs. For example, self-destructive behavior is a frequent sign of depression in teens. This may include anything from biting fingernails until they bleed to cutting oneself, driving recklessly, or abusing drugs or alcohol. Obsessions (fixations on a thought or an idea) and compulsions (uncontrollable and irrational urges to do something) also indicate depression.

Teenagers especially may experience poor performance at school (especially if this is in contrast to previous performance), disciplinary problems, feelings of anxiety and panic, unusual eating patterns, and physical symptoms such as stomachaches or headaches that are not explained by illness or other physical causes.

On the other hand, there are plenty of teens who are not depressed who show at least some of these symptoms. How can you tell if your feelings and moods (or those of a friend) are simply normal responses to the difficulties of adolescence or something more serious? A diagnosis of depression should be made only by a psychiatrist, psychologist, or other mental health professional. This checklist is not a substitute for an expert diagnosis, but it may help you determine whether or not you should consult a professional.

Photocopy this list and place a check mark next to every statement that describes you (or one of your friends) over the last two weeks or more:

Depression can express itself in many ways. You may be irritable and get annoyed easily. You may also behave in self-destructive ways, such as driving recklessly.

- I often feel sad for no reason.
- I cry easily.
- I have little or no hope that things will improve in the future.
- I get annoyed or angry easily.
- I feel numb inside and have difficulty caring about anyone, including myself.
- I get little pleasure from activities I used to enjoy.
- I have trouble concentrating in class or when doing homework or reading.

- I feel as though no one would notice if I were to disappear.
- I believe that I have let down my family, teachers, or friends.
- I have difficulty sleeping.
- I sleep a lot and have trouble getting out of bed.
- My appetite has decreased (or increased) lately.
- I doubt my ability to do anything well.
- I drink and/or use drugs more than I used to.
- I think about death and suicide often.

If you checked four or more of these statements, there is a good chance that you are depressed. You should discuss the test with a parent or guardian, then seek help from a qualified professional.

TEEN SUICIDE

Suicide is one of the leading causes of death among teenagers. Boys are more likely to commit suicide than girls; the suicide rate for boys is now five times greater than it was in 1950. Teens who are frequently depressed feel that their situation is hopeless and will never change. They may think that suicide is their only option. In addition, they may be influenced by classmates or celebrities who have committed suicide. Depression is not the only risk factor for suicide, and some teens who kill themselves are not suffering from depression at the time. The majority of depressed people do not commit suicide. Still, depression is probably the biggest cause of suicide among teens and adults.

Suicide is also a risk for people with bipolar disorder. In a manic state, someone who is bipolar may feel invincible and believe that he or she can "beat" death. This may lead the person to take dangerous risks such as playing with a gun or knife. When manic-depressives are in a depressed phase, they may feel hopeless, just as someone with unipolar depression does, and may decide to take their own life. If you or someone you know is thinking of suicide, seek help immediately. Contact a suicide hotline or talk to a trusted adult. Remember that depression is treatable and that even the worst situations can improve with time.

Suicide is permanent, and it is devastating to those who care about you. If you are concerned about a friend who may be suicidal, look for these warning signs:

- Symptoms of depression, such as feelings of hopelessness and guilt.
- Withdrawal from friends.
- Decreased activity level.
- Talking about relatives or others who have died.
- Talking about suicide—for example, discussing different potential methods or making statements such as "I wish I were dead."
- Increased use of drugs and/or alcohol.
- Engaging in risk-taking behavior such as reckless driving or shoplifting.
- Giving away possessions.
- Becoming suddenly cheerful with no explanation.

Teens may feel relieved or even elated if they have made a decision to commit suicide.

Talking About It

It is not always easy for parents to accept the idea that their children are depressed, and you may have trouble convincing your parents that you are in need of more help than they can give you. They may tell you that your feelings are just normal adolescent reactions and that they will pass. They may worry about being able to afford mental health care, or they may have negative ideas about psychiatry and psychology. They may even become angry at you for "complaining" about the way you feel or tell you that you have no reason to be depressed. If they react in one of these ways, it is most likely because they do not have accurate or up-to-date information about depression. They want you to be happy, but they may not have any idea how they can help you.

Whatever your parents' reaction, it is important to discuss your concerns with them. Try to stay calm and avoid becoming angry when you talk to them. Remember that they may feel guilty, anxious, and upset by your news. Prepare yourself beforehand by gathering information and, if possible, knowing what you would like them to do in order to help you feel better. Check the resources listed in the "For More Information" section at the end of this book to find free information about

It is good to talk about your feelings if you're depressed, especially with your parents. Expressing your emotions is a great way to combat negative feelings.

depression that you can read yourself and then share with your parents. You can also show your parents the previous checklist and your responses to it. If they are concerned about costs, remind them that free or inexpensive counseling is available in many communities and ask them to find out whether their health insurance, if they have it, will cover psychotherapy and other mental health treatment.

If you can help your parents understand that depression is an illness—a treatable illness—and that you want to feel better, chances are that they will be ready and eager to help you in any way they can. If they refuse to accept the idea that you are depressed, you may need to seek counseling on your own. Start with your school counselor, who may be able to help you find low-cost mental health care or suggest other ways for you to get help. Remember that even if your parents cannot or will not help, you are not alone; help is available.

THE RISK OF SUBSTANCE ABUSE

For many teens, adolescence is a time of experimentation and change. This can sometimes include experimenting with alcohol and other legal and illegal drugs. By the time they reach their mid-twenties, more than 70 percent of young people in the United States will have tried an illegal drug. Teens who have mood disorders are playing with fire if they abuse these substances, since many drugs can actually make depression or manic depression worse. Yet these teens are far more likely, on average, to experiment with drugs and alcohol and develop problems of substance abuse and addiction than teens who do not have psychological disorders. Similarly, teens who already have substance abuse problems are significantly more likely to develop mood disorders than their peers who do not use alcohol and other drugs.

THE GENDER FACTOR

About twice as many women as men suffer from depression. The ratio is roughly the same for teenagers. Why do so many more girls than boys become depressed? Researchers are not sure of the answer to this question. It is possible that adolescence is simply a harder time for girls than for boys. Adolescent girls face many pressures that do not affect boys to the same extent, including the pressure to look and dress a certain way, the pressure to be thin, and the pressure to be pretty.

Many teenage girls also face complex situations such as the risk of sexual abuse or harassment. These pressures and stresses do not automatically cause depression, but they may trigger it in a teenage girl whose brain chemistry makes her prone to depression.

Another possible explanation is that boys have trouble admitting to some of the common feelings associated with depression, such as sadness and low self-esteem. Boys are more likely to express their depression through aggressive, hostile, and even violent behavior, and boys who do so may be branded as troublemakers rather than being recognized as depressed. A girl who is depressed may cry uncontrollably and turn her unhappiness inward, directing it at herself. A boy who cries risks being ridiculed or accused of being un-masculine. Boys are thus more likely to turn their feelings outward; they may act out their depression by becoming involved in dangerous behavior such as drinking and driving or petty crime, or they may become physically aggressive, picking fights with their friends or classmates. Just because they express their depression differently from girls, however, does not mean that they are not depressed.

Substance abuse can be either a cause or an effect of depression or bipolar disorder, and people with both a substance abuse problem and a mood disorder need a special kind of professional help.

EATING DISORDERS AND DEPRESSION

Hundreds of thousands of teens suffer from eating disorders such as anorexia (self-starvation), bulimia (overeating and then vomiting or otherwise forcing food out of the body), and compulsive overeating. For many of these teens, depression is a key part of the eating disorder. Study after study has shown that among people with anorexia and bulimia, a large percentage—ranging from nearly half to more than 80 percent—could be diagnosed with some form of depression as well. Adults also suffer from eating disorders, but eating disorders are most common among people in their teens and twenties.

Like depression, eating disorders are much more likely to affect girls than boys, although the rate of eating disorders among boys is on the rise. In general the body changes and concerns about self-image that occur during adolescence seem to hit girls harder than boys. This may partly explain the fact that girls develop eating disorders so much more frequently. For many girls, the desire to be thin or meet an unrealistic physical ideal may become so intense that it leads to abnormal eating behaviors such as anorexia or bulimia.

Eating disorders, such as anorexia and bulimia, are not simply due to a desire to be thin. These conditions are often closely connected with depression and poor self-esteem.

Evidence suggests that people with mood disorders may be more likely to develop eating disorders than other people. Teens with eating disorders tend to have low self-esteem and be perfectionists about themselves, their appearance, and their achievements. These characteristics are also frequently found in people with depression and can be considered risk factors for both conditions.

Eating disorders are stressful both physically and emotionally, and depression can develop as a result of an eating disorder. Thus, eating disorders can be both causes and symptoms of mood disorders.

Fortunately eating disorders, like mood disorders, are almost always treatable. In some cases, notably among bulimics, antidepressants have been shown to be an effective treatment for eating disorders, allowing the therapist to treat both conditions at once. For others, it may be necessary to treat one disorder at a time, especially if the eating disorder is severe enough to be life threatening.

DEPRESSION IN CHILDREN

Adolescent depression is on the rise, and so is depression in children under the age of twelve. Until the late 1970s, psychiatrists did not acknowledge that children under twelve could suffer from depression. Before that, depression was regarded primarily as an emotional and psychological disorder, and children—especially young children—were not believed to be emotionally mature or developed enough to experience the disease. Today some health care professionals still resist the idea that young children can be depressed, perhaps in part because it is troubling to think of a child suffering psychological pain. This may make physicians or other professionals unwilling or unable to recognize the symptoms of depression in a child. Another difficulty in detecting the signs of depression in children is that they generally do not have the vocabulary or self-awareness to describe what they are feeling. Nonetheless, it is believed that as many as 1 percent of preschool-age children and 2 percent of school-age children are clinically depressed.

In children, depression does not show itself in quite the same way as it does in teenagers or adults. Children who are depressed often have trouble getting along with other children. They may act out their feelings by becoming aggressive to other kids or talking back to or arguing with teachers and parents. Some depressed children may refuse to do homework or chores or join the family at mealtimes. Others may complain of physical pain (stomachaches are a common complaint) or become fearful about everyday situations. Many children go through periods of rebellious or difficult behavior, but in depressed children, these behaviors are usually accompanied by a lack of interest in activities, low self-esteem, difficulty in concentrating, and changes in activity level, either to inactivity or hyperactivity.

Treatment for children with depression differs from treatment of teenagers and adults. Conventional talk therapy sessions with a psychotherapist may not be helpful, especially for young children, because children often cannot or will not describe and discuss their feelings. For this reason, many professionals who specialize in treating depressed children use play therapy, allowing children to use toys and dolls, music, or drawing to express themselves.

Family therapy, in which the child, his or her parents, and sometimes siblings all work with a psychotherapist, can also be helpful for children. In particularly long-lasting or severe cases, a psychiatrist may prescribe antidepressants, although this is uncommon for young children because the long-term side effects of antidepressants are not well known. In many cases, successful treatment of childhood depression can decrease the risk of a person experiencing further depressions later in life.

CHAPTER 2

Psychiatrists use the term "mood disorders" to distinguish them from other types of mental disorders, such as psychotic disorders (including schizophrenia) and personality disorders. Mood disorders are usually divided into two main types: unipolar and bipolar. Unipolar disorders are marked by a depressed mood, whereas bipolar disorder involves distinct manic ("up") and depressive ("down") phases.

Depression is often triggered by a specific event or series of events. It may strike for no apparent reason. No matter what the cause, however, people who are experiencing more than one of the following symptoms over a period of time (more than a few days or a week) may be suffering from depression and should seek help from a psychiatrist or other professional immediately:

- Feelings of extreme sadness, hopelessness, or worthlessness
- Loss of interest in routine pleasures and activities
- Sharp increase or decrease in appetite
- Decreased ability to concentrate
- Sleep disturbances: inability to fall asleep or to stay asleep, or excessive sleeping
- Thoughts of suicide

The American Psychiatric Association (APA) defines several different types of depression in its Diagnostic and Statistical Manual of Mental Disorders (usually referred to as the DSM-IV). All have similar symptoms; the differences among them are mainly in the degree of severity and how long the periods of depression last. Although major depression is considered the most severe of the types, the other forms of depression are also serious and require treatment. The distinctions among these types are subtle and are primarily useful for helping mental health professionals make a diagnosis and recommend appropriate treatment. They may also be helpful for patients. It is important to remember, though, that not everyone with depression will exactly match the diagnosis for one type or another. The definitions in the DSM-IV represent current psychiatric theories and research, and they will almost certainly change by the time the next edition is published. They should be viewed as guidelines rather than hard facts.

THE MOST SEVERE DEPRESSION

Major depressive disorder is the most severe of all the types of depression. People who are diagnosed with major depression have had most or all of the typical symptoms of depression—loss of interest in usual

Unusual sleeping patterns are a common symptom of depression. These include insomnia, the inability to sleep, or excessive sleeping.

activities; difficulty sleeping; fatigue and lack of energy; feelings of guilt, hopelessness, and low self-esteem; and changes in appetite—for a period of at least two weeks.

An episode of major depression may be brought on by stressful or painful events in someone's life, such as the breakup of a relationship or the death of a loved one. But major depression is different from a normal response to grief, and it will not be diagnosed if a patient's feelings of depression can be explained by a recent loss or stressful event. Major depression lasts longer, produces more intense feelings—not just the sorrow that you would expect to feel after a loss, but also a deep feeling of despair—and affects people more powerfully, often limiting their ability to function normally. Scientists cannot say for sure what makes one person more likely than another to slip into major depression after a loss or another difficult life event, but it is clear that some people are. This is probably because of differences in brain chemistry, but there are also other physical and psychological factors involved.

Some people may experience only one major depressive episode in their lives. Others may have episodes that recur every few years throughout their lives, and not all of these episodes will necessarily be triggered by a specific event. It appears that once the first episode occurs, a person is at greater risk for future depressive episodes than someone who has not experienced a severe depression. In some cases, successful treatment of a first depressive episode can help reduce the risk of future episodes.

Even if untreated, most episodes of major depression will eventually go away on their own. This can take months, however, and untreated depression can do long-term damage to people's lives— even lead to suicide—while it is active. Unfortunately only about one-third of people with depression ever seek treatment for their condition.

Some psychotherapists recognize three subtypes of major depression. The first is melancholic depression. The second is called atypical depression, which is a somewhat misleading name because it may be more common than melancholic depression. Atypical depression is usually characterized by weight gain and increased appetite rather than weight loss and decreased appetite (which are more typical of melancholic depression). People with atypical depression may find temporary relief from

Severe depression requires immediate attention by friends, family, and professionals. Left untreated, severe depression can cause major disruption to people's lives and relationships.

their condition if they are cheered up by attention and praise from others, which is not usually true for people with other subtypes of depression. Many experts believe that the differences between melancholic and atypical depression are due more to the different types of personalities of people with these two kinds of depression than to differences in the two illnesses themselves.

A third subtype, psychotic depression, is the least common type of depression. People who are suffering from psychotic depression experience delusions or hallucinations as well as depressive symptoms. They may describe themselves as confused or say that they feel as though they are "going crazy." They are also at great risk for suicide. The symptoms of psychotic depression are generally more obvious to patients and people around them than the symptoms of other forms of major depression. People with psychotic depression can almost always be helped by medication and psychotherapy; sometimes the psychiatric professional who is treating them will recommend hospitalization as well.

DYSTHYMIC DISORDER

Dysthymic disorder is similar to major depressive disorder, but the symptoms may be less intense, and they last longer. Dysthymic disorder, or dysthymia, is chronic; that is, it lasts for a significant amount of time. Dysthymia is diagnosed if a person has experienced the symptoms of depression for most of the day on a majority of days for a period of at least two years, or one year for children and teenagers.

People with dysthymic disorder are likely to describe themselves as rarely or never feeling happy. They may not be overwhelmed by their feelings, as someone with major depressive disorder might be, and they are less likely to be suicidal. Nonetheless, people with dysthymia take little pleasure in life, are frequently tired, and may be withdrawn or antisocial. Dysthymia often begins in childhood or adolescence, and some studies indicate that it is most common in children and young people who have parents or other close relatives who have experienced depression. It affects somewhat fewer people than major depressive disorder, although this may be because people with dysthymia are so used to the way they feel that they do not consider it abnormal and therefore do not seek treatment. They may consider their constant low mood to be an aspect of their personality rather than an illness that requires professional help.

People with dysthymic disorder often experience major depressive disorder either before or after their dysthymia first appears or even during the course of their dysthymia. They may also have other mental health problems, such as anxiety disorder. Like major depressive disorder, dysthymia affects about twice as many women as men. It is treated in the same way as major depression—usually with a combination of psychotherapy and antidepressant medication.

BIPOLAR DISORDER

There are approximately two million people with manic-depressive illness, or bipolar disorder, in the United States. People with this disorder alternate between periods of mania and periods of depression. The length of these manic and depressive periods vary from person to person. Manic periods usually last at least a week, and in some people, a manic period may last as long as six months. The depressive periods tend to be shorter and less frequent, but this is not true for everyone. Unlike other depressive mood disorders, bipolar disorder affects men and women in roughly equal numbers. It is especially common in people who have close relatives with the disorder, and the research that has been done so far indicates that there is a genetic component to bipolar disorder.

Everyone has mood swings, but people with bipolar disorder experience them in a much more extreme form. The signs of a manic episode include the following:

- Feeling invincible and capable of doing anything
- Having an inflated sense of self-esteem
- Restlessness
- Decreased need for sleep
- Irritability
- Difficulty concentrating; having too many thoughts at once
- Engaging in reckless behaviors such as spending sprees or dangerous driving

The signs of depression in people with bipolar disorder are similar to those found in people with unipolar (non-manic) depression. During a depressive episode, someone with bipolar disorder may feel hopeless and uncontrollably sad, may be considering suicide, and may sleep and eat more or less than usual. Not everyone with bipolar disorder experiences severe depressions, however. Some may feel normal or just slightly "down" between manic phases. Similarly, some people with bipolar disorder rarely experience the manic feeling but are frequently depressed. The manic periods that they do have tend to be relatively mild. This is usually referred to as type II bipolar disorder.

The time between manic and depressive periods also varies greatly from person to person. A small percentage of people who are bipolar experience what is known as rapid cycling between manic and depressive phases. In rapid cycling, four or more cycles of both mania and depression occur in a year, with no interval between mania and depression; that is, the end of a manic phase is marked by the beginning of a depression, and vice versa.

Bipolar disorder is a condition that generally responds very well to medication. The drug that is most commonly used to treat manic-depressive illness is lithium carbonate (usually just called lithium). Lithium usually stops manic episodes that are already under way, and it often seems to prevent future manic and depressive periods from occurring, as long as the patient continues to take the prescribed dose. The drug is frequently used in combination with psychotherapy to help the patient deal with stress and other problems that might trigger an episode of mania or depression. A medical professional may also prescribe tranquilizers to control or suppress a manic episode and/or antidepressants to help with depressive episodes. In a few cases in which the mania cannot be controlled, patients may be hospitalized to prevent them from harming themselves or others.

Bipolar disorder most often begins when people are in their teens or early twenties. Less commonly, it occurs in children younger than twelve. In children that age, bipolar disorder may be incorrectly diagnosed as attention deficit hyperactivity disorder (ADHD), with which it shares some symptoms, such as restlessness, inability to concentrate, and decreased need for sleep. Some people with bipolar disorder will experience only one or two manic-depressive episodes in their lives, and if these episodes are treated successfully, these people may never be troubled by the disease again. Others may require medication, with or without psychotherapy, throughout their lives. Fortunately, although the pharmacological and therapeutic treatments for this difficult condition do not always work, they are helpful in most cases.

In severe cases, people with bipolar disorder may feel so out of control that they consider suicide. Their behavior during a manic episode may get them into debt or legal trouble, and they may feel that they have no alternatives to suicide. Or they may become so depressed during their "down" periods that they feel there is no point in living. For this reason, it is especially important for people with the symptoms of bipolar disorder to seek professional help.

CYCLOTHYMIC DISORDER

Just as dysthymic disorder is a chronic but less severe version of major depression, cyclothymic disorder is a type of bipolar disorder characterized by repeated, less intense mood swings over a period of at least two years (one year for children and adolescents). The cyclothymic patient's manic moods are similar to those of someone with bipolar disorder, but the depressive moods are not as severe.

Cyclothymic disorder is usually treated with psychotherapy. In some cases that are especially long lasting, treatment with lithium may also be recommended.

OTHER MOOD DISORDERS

Psychiatrists recognize a number of other mood disorders that are similar to either unipolar or bipolar disorder. People may experience more than one of these disorders during their lifetime. These mood disorders are less severe than major depression, but all can be serious enough to require professional help. They include the following diagnoses.

ADJUSTMENT DISORDER WITH DEPRESSED MOOD

When someone has symptoms of depression in response to a stressful event such as a death in the family, a change in job or school, or a romantic breakup, they may be diagnosed as having adjustment disorder with depressed mood. Also called situational depression, this condition goes beyond the feelings of grief and sorrow that we would expect someone to have in response to a loss. Like more severe forms of depression, it includes feelings of hopelessness and guilt, as well as a loss of energy and a feeling of persistent fatigue. Though adjustment disorder with depressed mood is less intense than major depressive disorder and does not last as long as dysthymia, it resembles both of those disorders in its symptoms. Generally the symptoms of this disorder will diminish within six months of the stressful event. People who have an episode of this disorder may never experience another bout of depression, although in some cases, they will develop major depressive disorder or dysthymia later on.

SEASONAL AFFECTIVE DISORDER

Many people become depressed at certain times of year, most commonly in winter. These people may be suffering from seasonal affective disorder (SAD), a disorder that experts have only recently identified as a separate

The environment can also play a role in depression. People suffering from seasonal affective disorder (SAD) often feel worse when there is diminished sunlight during certain times of the year.

condition. People with SAD are not generally depressed, but at certain times of the year, they experience typical symptoms of mild depression, such as the following:

- Lack of energy.
- Loss of enthusiasm for usual activities.

- Trouble sleeping or sleeping too much.
- Changes in appetite. (Appetite usually increases in people with SAD.)

Recent research shows that SAD may be caused by an imbalance of neurotransmitters in the brain. This imbalance, most experts believe, is related to the amount of sunlight that people with SAD are exposed to. During the shorter days and longer nights of the fall and winter, people with SAD are exposed to less daylight, and this triggers their symptoms. This has not yet been conclusively proved; however, many people with the winter form of SAD find that light therapy is a successful treatment for their symptoms. In the most popular type of light therapy, SAD sufferers spend a period of time each day in front of full-spectrum lights (a type of fluorescent lightbulb). Used in combination with antidepressant medication, light therapy seems to be an effective and safe treatment for many people with winter SAD. The form of SAD that affects people in spring and summer is less well known, and no specific treatment has been developed for it.

Not surprisingly, the winter form of SAD occurs more frequently in the northern United States and Canada, where winter days are especially short, than in the southern United States. In Alaska, for example, as much as 9 or 10 percent of the population may have SAD, and one study done at a clinic in northern Canada suggested that 20 percent of the population of that region suffers from SAD.

Many people suffering from depression turn to abusing substances such as drugs and alcohol. While these chemicals may make users feel better temporarily, they often create more damage.

SUBSTANCE-INDUCED MOOD DISORDER

A substance-induced mood disorder is one in which the change in mood is directly caused by the effects of a substance. Substances that can induce a mood disorder include the following:

- Alcohol
- Illegal drugs such as heroin, cocaine, and marijuana

- Legal drugs that are abused, for example, prescription medications that are taken for longer periods or in higher doses than prescribed
- Prescription and nonprescription (over-the-counter) medications, including antihistamines, medicines for heart disease, muscle relaxants, pain relievers, and others that the user takes as prescribed
- Toxic chemicals such as paint, toluene (the chemical in spray cans), and others that are deliberately abused
- Toxic chemicals that a person is exposed to accidentally, including pesticides, carbon monoxide, and others

The symptoms of a substance-induced mood disorder usually resemble those of other mood disorders such as major depression, dysthymic disorder, or bipolar disorder, but substance-induced mood disorders are treated as a separate condition because they have a single, identifiable cause. These disorders must be treated somewhat differently from mood disorders that have organic physical and psychological causes.

PREMENSTRUAL DYSPHORIC DISORDER

Many girls and women are familiar with premenstrual syndrome (PMS), a set of various physical and emotional symptoms that affect women in the week or so before their monthly menstrual period begins.

There are other emotional disorders that sometimes accompany depression and may resemble depression. Anxiety and panic disorders and phobias are the most common of these. People with anxiety disorders may feel anxious, tense, and nervous for no specific reason (generalized anxiety disorder), or they may have panic attacks at specific times or in response to particular events (panic disorder). People with phobias generally fear specific situations or events, such as crowds (agoraphobia) or enclosed spaces (claustrophobia). The fear and tension that people with anxiety disorders and phobias experience can be paralyzing. In addition, they may feel guilty or ashamed of their anxiety, which they feel is abnormal and may be a sign that they are "crazy." These factors, along with the added stress of dealing with them, can lead to depression.

On the other hand, people with depression sometimes develop anxieties and phobias as a consequence of their depression. They may become extremely self-conscious about their social skills and ability to deal with others. Many depressed people are withdrawn and isolated, and this may develop into a genuine fear of leaving the house. It is not always easy to tell which came first, the depression or the anxiety. It is important for a therapist to determine the underlying causes of anxiety and depression and to treat each disorder appropriately.

ACCOMPANYING DISORDERS

These symptoms may include bloating, weight gain, tenderness in the breasts, sadness or irritability, and fatigue. A small number of women experience the emotional symptoms of PMS so severely that they are unable to function normally. They generally sleep excessively, feel despondent, have trouble sleeping, or become irritable and even aggressive. Psychiatrists have identified this condition as a mood disorder called premenstrual dysphoric disorder, or PMDD. PMDD is not at all common; it affects less than 5 percent of all girls and women who menstruate.

DEPRESSION AS A SIDE EFFECT

Depression is a common side effect of a serious physical illness such as cancer or heart disease. People with illnesses that are difficult to treat and carry a significant risk of death often become deeply depressed and must receive treatment for their depression as well as for the physical aspects of their illness. Some illnesses also cause symptoms that resemble depression but are not caused by a depressive disorder. When these illnesses are treated, the depressive symptoms go away.

Anyone who is seeking professional help for depression should also seek medical advice to make sure that the depression is not being caused by a medical condition. Specifically, someone with no prior history of depression who begins experiencing symptoms such as lethargy, fatigue, loss of interest in activities, and weight

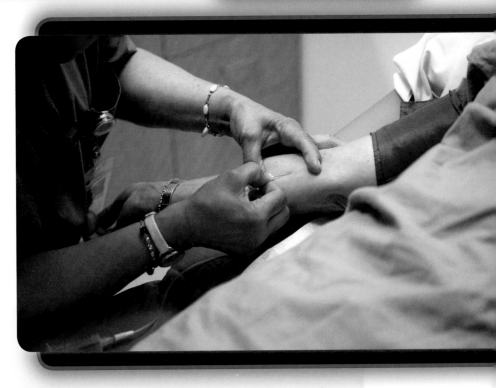

There may be a valid medical reason for one's depression, including illness or a thyroid imbalance. It's important to check with a doctor, who can administer a blood test.

gain should have a blood test to check his or her thyroid level. Hypothyroidism, or low function of the thyroid gland, can cause many of the same symptoms as depression and should be ruled out as a cause of these symptoms before a patient seeks treatment for depression. An over-functioning thyroid, which causes hyperthyroidism, can also produce symptoms that resemble those caused by depression, including inability to concentrate, trouble sleeping, and irritability.

ASK DR. JAN, PSYCHOLOGIST

First name: Marie

Question: So many people have told me that I'm tough and strong, but I also deal with depression and hold in my emotions. How can I deal with my depression and not hurt my friendships?

Answer: For many children and adolescents, depression can actually look like anger. Family and friends often misinterpret it as being mean or oppositional, not realizing that the person is actually struggling with underlying depression. In most cases where people have anger management issues, it is because they are not expressing their feelings or, as you say, they are holding in their emotions. When we don't deal with and express negative feelings, they don't just go away. They build and build, like a pressure cooker, until sooner or later the person explodes. That's why others see their response as a major overreaction, because in addition to the current situation, they are also venting unexpressed feelings from many preceding events.

The best way to deal with your depression is to express your feelings and not hold them in. While others see you as tough and strong, believe it or not you need to be more assertive. Many people believe they are assertive when they are actually aggressive, which is very different. Being assertive means expressing your feelings while being respectful of others' feelings. A good structure to use is an assertive statement, where you first respectfully say how you think the other person is feeling and only then share your own feelings. For example, if your parent takes your cell phone as a consequence of poor grades, you might say, "I know that you feel disappointed in my grades, but I feel really angry that you're taking my phone away." While speaking assertively may not get your phone back, it allows you to express your feelings in a healthy way that won't get you into more trouble. This same technique can help you with your friends and peers, too.

Ask a Question

Do you have a question that you would like answered? E-mail your question to Dr. Jan at drjan@rosenpub.com. If your question is selected, it will appear on the Teen Health & Wellness Web site in "Dr. Jan's Corner."

If you have an urgent question on a health or wellness issue, we strongly encourage you to call a hotline to speak to a qualified professional or speak to a trusted adult, such as a parent, teacher, or guidance counselor. You can find hotlines listed in the For More Information section of this book, or at www. teenhealthandwellness.com/static/hotlines.

Depression is a complex disease to understand and to live with. It has become increasingly common in the past forty or fifty years, and research suggests that people who develop depressive disorder have their first bout of depression at an earlier age than they did in the past.

These facts can be explained in part by increased awareness of depression among medical and psychiatric professionals as well as among the general public. Despite this increase in awareness, only about one-third of people with depression are likely to seek treatment for it. Failure to seek treatment may be due to a variety of causes, including the following:

- Embarrassment or shame at being depressed; feeling that depression is a sign of weakness or "craziness"
- Misdiagnosis or lack of recognition of symptoms by health care providers
- Refusal by a patient to admit to feelings of depression
- Distrust of psychiatric treatments
- Belief that depression is incurable or that it is simply an unchangeable part of the patient's personality

The good news is that depression can be treated successfully in a majority of cases. As awareness of depression grows, more and more sufferers will seek and find treatments for their condition, and with luck, the idea that depression is something to be ashamed of or embarrassed about will eventually disappear.

1. How long do I have to be depressed before I should seek help?

2. Is it normal to be depressed once in a while?

3. What are the common symptoms of bipolar disorder?

4. I have a friend who may be depressed. Should I try to help her myself or find her professional help?

5. Is it legal to carry around my prescription medication that I take for depression?

6. Does my depression mean that I'm crazy?

7. Is the information I tell my therapist confidential?

8. What if I don't want to take medication for my depression? Are there natural remedies?

9. What lifestyle changes can I make to manage my depression?

10. Will my depression get worse if it goes untreated?

10 GREAT QUESTIONS TO ASK YOUR DOCTOR

To understand the current theories about how depression originates in the brain, it is necessary to understand a little bit about how the brain works. In simple terms, the electrical signals that determine our moods and behavior are transmitted between nerve cells in our brains. The signals go from one cell to another across thin strands called axons, which extend between the cells. The signals are not transferred directly from one cell to another; instead, when one cell receives an electrical signal, its axon "fires," producing a chemical called a neurotransmitter. This chemical reaches the next cell, which causes its axon to produce a neurotransmitter that sends the signal to another cell, and so on.

The neurotransmitters that seem to have the most to do with depression are serotonin, norepinephrine, and dopamine. Some studies have shown that depressed people have lower levels of these neurotransmitters in their brains. Scientists theorize that in depressed people, the amount of neurotransmitter that is left between the cells after the axon has fired is reabsorbed quickly by the first cell. Certain types of anti-depressants work by keeping this re-absorption from taking place, making a greater supply of the neurotransmitter available to the brain. Other medications seem to accomplish this by causing cells to release larger amounts of neurotransmitters, increasing the strength of the signal that is sent to the next cell.

If low levels of neurotransmitters were the only physical explanation for depression in all depressed people, we would expect that antidepressants that control the re-absorption or production of these chemicals would work equally well in all depressed patients. This is not true, however, and scientists recognize that the exact links between brain chemistry and depression are not yet precisely known or understood. More research must be done before any of the current theories can be accepted as valid or rejected as inaccurate.

Some scientists believe that a person's brain chemistry can actually be altered by a loss or other painful life event. This theory would help explain the sudden onset of depression in someone who has never shown signs of having a mood disorder before. Again, more research on this theory is needed before scientists can say conclusively whether or not it is correct. Further studies of other neurotransmitters and their role in affecting moods will also help scientists understand how brain chemistry and depression are related.

Some scientists believe that hormones—substances secreted by glands in our bodies—are involved in determining whether or not a person will become depressed. Hormones regulate many of our bodies' functions, including reproduction and growth, so it may be reasonable to think that they could be involved in determining our mental state. We do know that the thyroid gland can affect mood if it does not function properly.

DEPRESSION AND ILLNESS

Illnesses have been linked to depression. People with mononucleosis, a common and relatively minor disease that is caused by a virus, often feel fatigued, restless, and unhappy as a result of their illness. Some scientists believe that mononucleosis leads patients to develop depression, although a recent study found no link between the two. Similar theories exist about chronic fatigue syndrome, which is caused by the same virus as mononucleosis, but again, there is no reliable evidence that there is a link between this disease and depression. Certain types of hepatitis, which is a viral illness that affects liver function, have also been associated with depression. Life-threatening illnesses such as cancer and heart disease can make people depressed as well. People who are suffering from these illnesses often require treatment for their depression at the same time.

Depressive symptoms may also be a sign of certain diseases that affect the brain and the central nervous system. Parkinson's disease, Lyme disease, epilepsy, anemia, and multiple sclerosis are among the diseases that produce symptoms similar to those caused by a depressive disorder. Certain medications used to treat various physical illnesses may cause depressive symptoms, too. These medications range from over-the-counter antihistamines such as Benadryl, which is used to treat allergies, to medicines prescribed for high blood pressure and arthritis. When this is the case, switching to a different type of medication will usually eliminate the depressive symptoms.

If someone's thyroid is underactive and therefore produces too little thyroid hormone—a condition called hypothyroidism—the person will have little energy, will gain weight, will be tired all the time, and may show other depressive symptoms. An overactive thyroid, which causes a condition called hyperthyroidism, can also produce depressive or manic-depressive symptoms, such as restlessness, sleep disturbances, irritability, and excitability.

YOUR GENES

Is depression in our genes? Genes, located within the cells of our body, contain information that we inherit from each of our parents. Genes are responsible for determining features such as our eye and hair color, and they probably play a part in deciding many other things about us, including our personalities, our tastes, and our interests. They also determine whether or not we will develop certain diseases. Genes have been shown to affect the likelihood of a person having cancer, heart disease, and asthma, for example. In some cases, a health condition can be traced to a particular gene. There is, for example, a specific gene that causes Down syndrome, a mild form of mental retardation. When a gene (or group of genes) is directly linked to a disease or condition, it becomes easier for researchers to look for a cure.

Unfortunately there does not appear to be a single gene that causes depression. That does not mean that there is no genetic component to depression, however.

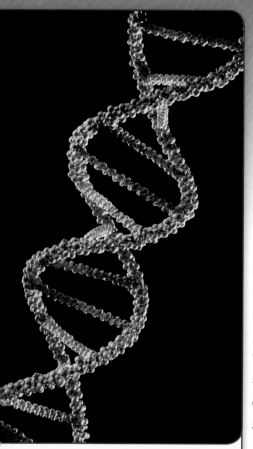

While there is still no conclusive evidence that genetics plays a direct role in depression, many experts believe that one's genetic makeup, along with other factors, plays a role in depression.

According to current research, it appears that certain genes cause people to be more likely to develop depression. The presence of these genes does not, by itself, automatically guarantee that someone will become depressed, but it increases the likelihood that this will happen. The environment in which a person grows up, the experiences he or she has throughout life, and other factors all influence that person's mental health in addition to genetics. The NIMH is sponsoring research into the exact link between genetics and mood disorders.

Other mental disorders, such as schizophrenia, seem to have a strong genetic component. Bipolar disorder also appears to be hereditary (passed on from one generation to another), probably more so than unipolar depression. Someone who has a close family member—parent, grandparent, brother, or sister—with bipolar disorder is significantly more likely to become bipolar than someone with no family history of the disease. As with depression, however, having a bipolar parent does not mean that someone will definitely develop bipolar disorder. It simply means that the risk of becoming bipolar is greater for that person than for someone without a family history of the disorder.

EMOTIONAL CAUSES

For many depressed people, the first experience of depression occurs during or after a period of stress or emotional trauma (a painful or otherwise difficult event). The most common sort of trauma that is associated with the beginning of a depressive episode is a loss of some kind. There are obvious examples of losses—such as the death of a parent or other close family member, or the breakup of a romantic relationship—as well as some slightly less obvious examples, such as leaving a home or familiar city, experiencing parents' divorce, or growing apart from an old friend.

Sadness, grief, and a sense of emptiness are natural responses to these events, and most people experience them for a period of time after the event. That period of time varies greatly for each individual, and there is no "right" amount of time that is an appropriate grieving period. For some people, however, the sadness does not fade over time. Instead it deepens and turns into major depression. What makes these people unable to move past their grief?

According to the biological theory of depression, people who become depressed as a result of a stressful or traumatic event have different brain chemistry from people who are able to move on after a period of grieving. They may also have a genetic tendency to become depressed or a hormonal imbalance that makes them less able to cope with difficult circumstances. The difference in brain chemistry may have been present all along, or it may actually have been caused by the event. This is currently the subject of a great deal of research. Similarly, some experts believe that there are biological differences in how various people handle stress, and there is some physical evidence that this is true.

LOW SELF-ESTEEM

Mental health professionals who look at depression as an emotional as well as biochemical disease might say that the person who is unable to get beyond grief suffers from low self-esteem. People who do not have any belief in themselves and lack a sense of their own value may depend too much on the important people and relationships in their lives. They rely on those people to give them a sense of self-worth rather than getting that sense from their own achievements and behavior. If they lose one of those important relationships, through death, a breakup, or other circumstances, they may also lose whatever sense of self-esteem they have. They begin to feel worthless, hopeless, and often guilty—in other words, they become depressed.

It is also possible and fairly common for people to become depressed for no apparent reason, without having recently experienced any sort of stress or trauma. Lack of self-esteem is often at the root of this type of depression as well. People with low self-esteem frequently believe that they do not deserve to be happy. It is very hard to feel happy if you do not believe yourself to be deserving of happiness.

But what causes low self-esteem? There are a wide variety of causes, but most of them have to do with how a person was treated in childhood. Children who are abused, for example, whether sexually, physically, or emotionally, almost never have healthy self-esteem. Someone they trust and depend on—a parent, another close relative, or another trusted adult—has hurt them. Rather than being angry at the abuser, these children often

Low self-esteem is characterized by feelings of low self-worth. These feelings can contribute to, or even cause, depression because of the constant sense of hopelessness.

begin to believe that they must have done something to deserve the abuse or that they are simply "bad" and in

Low self-esteem can date back to childhood and be caused by abusive or overbearing parents. These feelings can last well into adulthood after the parents are gone.

need of punishment. This may be reinforced by the abuser, who may tell the child that he or she is no good and deserves the treatment being given. If the abuse continues, the child is at great risk of becoming severely depressed.

Sometimes the damage to a person's self-esteem comes in much subtler ways. Parents who ridicule or criticize a child's behavior, thoughts, and ideas can damage that child's self-esteem and discourage him or her from becoming happy and successful. Parents who set unreasonably high standards for their children may in turn cause the child to set those same unreasonable standards for himself or herself later in life and to feel like a failure if those standards are not met. Teachers who tell children they are not smart enough, coaches who tell them that they are poor athletes, even older siblings who tease and make fun of younger ones without balancing out the teasing with affection and support can cause or contribute to a child's belief that he or she is worthless and unimportant.

Parents do not usually intend to damage a child's self-esteem, and some children can develop strong self-esteem with or without encouragement from their parents. Parents may act out of good intentions that have unfortunate results; for example, believing that they are making their children stronger by criticizing them. Depression and low self-esteem cannot simply be blamed on parents; many other factors help determine whether or not someone will be depressed. Nonetheless, much of our behavior and emotions as adolescents and adults is shaped by how we feel and how we are treated as children, and most people with depression can trace the root causes of their depression to their childhoods.

Some people seem to be more likely to be affected by these threats to self-esteem than others. Again, this may be because of an inherited tendency, brain chemistry, or a combination of factors. Not every child with poor self-esteem will eventually become depressed, but lack of self-esteem does often seem to go hand-in-hand with depression. Fortunately self-esteem can be rebuilt over time, usually with the help of a psychotherapist or other professional.

LONELINESS

There is a vast difference between being alone in a room and feeling lonely. The former is a temporary, perhaps voluntary situation that doesn't necessarily carry with it any impact, fleeting or lasting. Technology has allowed us to stay connected with friends and family, even when we are physically alone in a room or moving among strangers. You may be alone, yet engaged in conversation on message boards, in chat rooms, or via e-mail, text messages, and cell phones.

However, loneliness, as opposed to being alone, is an emotional state that people of all ages can feel whether by themselves, with their romantic partner, hanging out with friends, or surrounded by a large crowd. It is an emotional state, not a physical one. It's a feeling of solitariness, isolation, and lack of warmth and love that is not necessarily dependent upon how many people are around you. Left untreated, loneliness can lead to other emotional and psychological problems. In fact, some studies indicate that a quarter of the U.S. population considers themselves lonely at any given time.

Loneliness is the awareness that you are not feeling connected to peers or family or the world around you. This can happen in overt ways, such as being excluded from a group or feeling unloved by those in your social circle. You may feel alienated from your surroundings (either familiar ones or new ones). You may think that there is no one with whom you can or want to share your thoughts and feelings. You may sense that you are alone with no alternatives. When caught up in these kinds of emotions, try to remember that feeling a certain way isn't the same as being a certain way. You may feel alone, unloved, and without hope, but that doesn't mean you truly are alone, unloved, or without hope.

The pioneering sociologist at the University of Massachusetts, Dr. Robert Weiss, noted two larger distinctions among types of loneliness. He distinguished between social loneliness—the feeling of having no attachment to any social community or network—and emotional loneliness—the absence of intimate attachments to individuals. Weiss also wrote that loneliness and depression are not the same condition, although one can lead to the other. Lonely people will lament their situation but often seek remedies, whereas depressed people often feel they're done trying and may just give up.

Similarly, loneliness can often be confused with shyness. Being shy may involve holding back from approaching others for fear of being rejected, looking foolish, making some kind of mistake, or otherwise making yourself vulnerable and exposed to social failure or criticism. This can be made even more difficult if the social setting is intimidating, such as a crowded party full of strangers. In some ways loneliness is a mourning of something that has been lost—a former sense of connection and intimacy—whereas shyness is a hesitancy surrounding the forming of a connection. It's almost an anticipatory fear of not forming a connection in the first place, rather than losing a connection that had been formed.

A University of Chicago report indicates that loneliness can be a genetic trait, meaning that if someone in your family has suffered from loneliness, you may be more susceptible to it. In addition, those who are chronically lonely also tend to exhibit signs of chronic depression and anxiousness, dubbed the "unholy trinity" by the report.

These three can drag you into a downward spiral if you do not seek help. At the very least, try to overcome your sense of loneliness and isolation to reach out to friends and family members and talk about what you're experiencing. Also consider seeking professional help from a therapist or psychologist. He or she can help you explore your feelings and what is causing them and give you concrete suggestions for how to break out of your unhappiness and alter behavior and thought patterns that may be holding you back. If the psychologist suspects your loneliness and depression are chemical in nature—the result of a chemical imbalance—he or she may be able to help you get prescriptions for medication that will restore the proper chemical balance and relieve your symptoms.

If you are experiencing suicidal thoughts as a result of your loneliness and/or depression, call a suicide hotline or 911 immediately. Then make an appointment with a professional therapist who will help you confront your feelings and find a way to address them in a more positive and effective way that will keep you safe and protect your health.

CHAPTER 4

Many people who struggle with depression turn to drugs and alcohol in the hope that these substances will make them feel better. Although some drugs and alcohol may make people feel temporarily happy or energetic, these substances actually make the symptoms of depression worse. Nonetheless, the belief that alcohol or illegal drugs will get rid of their depression leads some people to abuse these substances, often to the point of addiction (a physical and emotional need for a substance).

Similarly, using alcohol or other drugs to the extent that they interfere with a person's day-to-day functioning at work, at school, or at home can cause depression or make an existing mood disorder worse. Addiction to alcohol or other drugs is considered a disease. It is not a sign of weak character; rather, it is a disorder with physical and psychological causes. People who have this disease and do not undergo treatment may develop depression or another mood disorder.

To make matters more complicated, substance abuse problems can mask the symptoms of depression. This is partly because the symptoms of a substance abuse problem may be much more obvious, both to the affected person

While substance abuse can make feelings of depression even worse, the feeling of euphoria that drugs and alcohol create can mask the symptoms of depression when they should be treated.

and to professionals, than the symptoms of depression. People who are attempting to end their addiction often experience the symptoms of depression as they go through physical and psychological withdrawal from the drug. Although this depression is usually temporary, lasting only a month or two, it can further complicate a patient's diagnosis.

There are three basic types of relationships between mood disorders and substance abuse disorders:

- The mood disorder and the substance abuse problem are two separate disorders that have developed because of similar biological and psychological causes. This is often the case, for example, with people who are victims of abuse as well as for people who develop psychological disorders after other traumatic events.
- The mood disorder is caused by the substance abuse. Both abuse of and withdrawal from certain drugs, including alcohol, cocaine, heroin, and amphetamines, can trigger the development of a psychological disorder. Some substances actually cause a change in brain chemistry that results in depression or mania.
- The substance abuse is caused by the mood disorder. This may occur because a depressed or bipolar person is trying to heal his or her own symptoms with drugs or alcohol. It can also be a result of self-destructive impulses. The latter is particularly common among young people (especially those with bipolar disorder), who are generally more likely to engage in risky behavior than adults are. According to a study by the NIMH, depressed people are twice as likely as people without mood disorders to abuse drugs, although they are not significantly more likely to abuse alcohol.

DUAL DIAGNOSIS

The combination of substance abuse and mood disorders is often referred to as a dual disorder, and people

who are diagnosed with both are said to have a dual diagnosis (although in some cases, people have more than two disorders). "Dual diagnosis" is a term that doctors in all areas of medicine use to refer to patients who have more than one medical condition at the same time. In the psychiatric field, it has come to mean that the patient has a substance-related disorder and another psychological disorder. To treat a patient with a dual diagnosis, a health care professional must determine whether the substance abuse is the underlying cause of the mood disorder, a symptom of it, or an independent condition. Both disorders must be treated for the patient to recover from either one, but the treatment approach is different for every patient with a dual diagnosis.

Dual diagnosis is a special cause of concern for teenagers. A study conducted at Columbia University found that among people between the ages of nine and seventeen, those who had substance abuse problems and depression or bipolar disorder were about eight times more likely to attempt suicide than those without either disorder, and about 3 percent more likely than those with depression alone. Adolescence is a time when many people experiment with drugs and alcohol, and teenagers may be especially likely to turn to substance abuse as a means of dealing with depression. The link between substance abuse, depression, and suicide risk is a critical

People whose depression and substance abuse reinforce one another are said to have a dual diagnosis. Withdrawal from drugs or alcohol can heighten the feelings of depression.

one to recognize in teen boys, who have higher rates of both addiction and suicide than girls of the same age.

There is no one type of dual diagnosis. Substance abuse disorders can exist alongside a number of psychological disorders, including schizophrenia, personality disorders, and anxiety disorders as well as depression and manic depression. In some cases, the substance abuse problem is more severe than the psychological disorder; in others, the opposite is true. And in some cases, the two disorders are equally severe and affect the individual equally. Thus there is no all-purpose treatment for dual disorders; each one must be evaluated and approached individually.

How common is dual diagnosis? Approximately one-third of people with psychiatric disorders will abuse alcohol or other drugs at some point in their lives, compared to less than half that percentage of people without psychiatric disorders. For people with substance abuse disorders, more than half will experience the symptoms of some type of psychological disorder—usually depression, personality disorders, or anxiety disorders—during their lives. This includes people with an underlying psychological disorder as well as people with substance-induced mood disorders and people whose psychological problems are only a symptom of their addiction.

Not everyone who uses or abuses alcohol or other drugs will become addicted. Addiction is a complex disease, and experts are not entirely certain why some people develop addictions and others do not, even if both use the same substances in the same amounts.

It is never a good idea to use illegal drugs or misuse legal ones. If you use alcohol or other drugs but are not physically dependent on them, you may think that you have your drug use under control. That is not always the case, however. It is possible to have a substance abuse disorder without being an addict. The use of alcohol and other drugs becomes abuse if:

- It has a negative impact on your job, home life, schoolwork, or extracurricular activities such as sports
- You become unable to function normally
- You frequently put yourself in dangerous situations while under the influence of the substance
- You continue to use the substance despite the concerns of friends, family members, teachers, or employers
- You commit crimes or are arrested while under the influence of the substance

If any of the previous statements are true for you, you may have a substance abuse problem; if two or more are true, you almost certainly do. You should seek help from a qualified substance abuse counselor immediately. If you are not certain about how to find help, check the "For More Information" section at the end of this book. There are numerous free and confidential clinics, hotlines, and other services that can get you started on the road to recovery.

DO I HAVE A SUBSTANCE ABUSE PROBLEM?

What is clear is that some people are physically and psychologically predisposed to becoming addicted. For these people, the existence of a mood disorder alongside the addiction becomes a vicious cycle that is difficult to escape.

BIPOLAR DISORDER

Dual diagnosis is especially common among people with bipolar disorder. A study by the NIMH found that people with bipolar disorder are two to three times as likely to abuse drugs or alcohol as people with unipolar depression and nearly seven times more likely than people without mood disorders. This means that more than half of people with bipolar disorder will abuse alcohol or other drugs at some time. This is a dangerous percentage, especially because substance abuse has been shown to make bipolar disorder worse, causing more frequent and severe manic and depressive episodes and often causing rapid cycling back and forth between phases. Certain substances in particular—notably cocaine, amphetamines, and other drugs that have a stimulating effect—are likely to trigger manic episodes.

In treating bipolar disorder, therapists may focus on preventing substance abuse problems before they can begin. The likelihood that a person with bipolar disorder will develop addictions increases dramatically after the first episode of mania, so addressing the potential problem of addiction as early as possible after the patient is first diagnosed with bipolar disorder is an important part of therapy.

TREATMENT

Treatment for dual diagnosis presents some unique problems for mental health professionals. For example, the most common type of treatment for substance abuse is based on a twelve-step program. This type of program, originally developed by the founder of Alcoholics Anonymous (AA), centers around regular group meetings with other people who are also recovering from problems with the same substance. People in twelve-step programs usually have a sponsor—another member of the group who has been in recovery longer.

These meetings are interactive and participatory, which may be extremely difficult for people who are severely depressed. People with depression may benefit more from one-on-one sessions with a psychotherapist, as well as treatment with antidepressant drugs (in some cases), than from traditional substance abuse treatment. Once the depressive symptoms have been controlled, the patient may be more receptive to the twelve-step approach to treatment.

Similarly, treating a mood disorder with medication can present risks for people who are substance abusers because they may over-medicate themselves (take too much medication) or continue to use drugs or alcohol while taking antidepressants, which can cause

Talking about your problems in a group, whether in therapy or just with friends, can help you deal with substance abuse problems and depression.

dangerous side effects. Substance abuse counselors have traditionally been opposed to the use of antidepressants or other medications for psychological disorders because they believed that a person who has a history of substance abuse should avoid any mood-altering drug, even potentially helpful ones. As more and more studies appear that indicate that the use of antidepressants can be very beneficial in treating patients with dual diagnosis, however, this resistance to prescribing medication for substance abuse patients is beginning to fade.

Although most antidepressants are not usually abused, since they do not produce a high or other immediate effect, many of them can enhance the "up" or

"down" effect of illegal drugs. Doctors who prescribe antidepressants for patients with a dual diagnosis must carefully monitor their patients to make sure that they do not abuse alcohol or drugs while taking the antidepressants. People with a dual diagnosis will usually benefit most from a combination of the right medication and talk therapy. Medication alone is not always effective for these patients. This is especially true for manic-depressives with problems of substance abuse or addiction.

Treatment of dual diagnosis can be complicated in practical terms, too. The psychotherapist who is treating the mood disorder may not be trained in treating substance abuse and addiction. Similarly, the substance abuse counselor may not have the experience or training to recognize the symptoms of a mood disorder. If this is the case, the therapist must work together with the substance abuse counselor to ensure that neither type of therapy conflicts with the other.

MYTH

My friends will think I'm crazy because I'm depressed.

FACT

Depression is a condition that nearly everyone experiences at one time or another. It is likely that your friends have gone through a similar depression to yours and will understand that it is a common side effect of this dynamic time in your life.

MYTH

I will never get over my depression.

FACT

Depression is a highly manageable and treatable condition. Every year, new therapies and medications are being introduced that can help you better manage and even eliminate depression.

MYTH

All depressed people have a negative outlook on life.

FACT

While having a negative view of the world can contribute to depression, the condition is much more complex. Depression is known to be the result of a number of factors, including personal outlook, but also genetics, environment, and events in one's life.

MYTHS AND FACTS

CHAPTER 5

ANTIDEPRESSANTS

Antidepressants are medications prescribed by doctors to treat depression and other disorders, such as panic and eating disorders and anxiety. Currently, more than twenty different antidepressants are available for adults and teens. Most can be taken as a capsule, tablet, or liquid. The U.S. Food and Drug Administration (FDA) regulates antidepressants and all other prescription medications.

Antidepressants are not stimulants. They do not make you feel overly excited, happy, or peppy. Antidepressants reduce the amount of excessive depression that you were feeling. They help you feel the way you did before you became depressed.

Antidepressants are commonly used in the United States. In 2008, the Agency for Healthcare Research and Quality reported that prescriptions for antidepressants increased from 154 million in 2002 to 170 million in 2005. Also in 2008, *Scientific American* reported that 5 percent of men and 11 percent of women were taking antidepressants. The use of antidepressants among people ages ten to nineteen continues to increase.

HOW ANTIDEPRESSANTS WORK

Researchers are not exactly sure how antidepressants change the chemistry of the brain.

Your brain is made up of billions of neurons that communicate with one another. Neurons pass messages to other neurons by releasing many different types of chemical substances called neurotransmitters. The main neurotransmitters that antidepressants affect are serotonin, norepinephrine, and, to a lesser extent, dopamine.

Neurotransmitters are released from storage in small "bubbles" called vesicles, which are located at the ends of neurons (nerve cells). These biochemicals cross the gaps between neurons, called synapses, and then bind to neurotransmitter receptors on nearby neurons. Messages that move from neuron to neuron can be about thoughts, emotions, behavior, body temperature, appetite, or other body functions. The types and amounts of neurotransmitters control how neurons communicate in the brain. When neurotransmitters finish their work, the sending neuron usually reabsorbs them in a process called reuptake. Then the neurotransmitters can be released again later.

Sometimes the reuptake of serotonin or norepinephrine occurs too soon. As a result, the brain does not have enough of the neurotransmitter. This can cause depression. Each type of antidepressant works differently. Some antidepressants slow the reuptake process of serotonin or norepinephrine in the brain. Other antidepressants interact directly with the receptors that release these neurotransmitters. In all cases, antidepressants cause an increase in the levels of serotonin or norepinephrine that stick around in the synapses. This process allows more neurotransmitters to interact with their receptors, which generally improves people's moods.

The receptors take some time to adapt in different ways as the levels of neurotransmitters increase. It is not known if the number of receptors increases or the ability of neurotransmitters to bind to their receptors increases. Perhaps it is a combination of the two. Researchers think that the changes in the receptors cause mood to improve, but they do not completely understand yet how this happens. Receptors usually take from two to four weeks to adjust. This means it takes that long, or a little longer, for most antidepressants to take full effect in the body.

POSSIBLE RISK OF SUICIDAL BEHAVIOR

When doctors prescribe an antidepressant for teens, their first choice is often a type of antidepressant called selective serotonin reuptake inhibitors (SSRIs). Most teens have few side effects when using SSRIs. If side effects occur, they usually disappear within a month. Compared to other types of antidepressants, SSRIs are less likely to be harmful if teens take an overdose. This is important because teens with depression are already at an increased risk for suicide.

Some people think that the use of antidepressants increases the risk of suicide in children and teens. The FDA has analyzed 24 past studies of about 4,400 teens and children who had taken antidepressants. No suicides had occurred in the studies. However, the agency

Antidepressants come in many forms, including selective serotonin reuptake inhibitors (SSRIs). It is important to seek a doctor's advice and prescription regarding which antidepressants to take or whether to take them at all.

stated that SSRIs may cause a very small proportion of teens to be at an increased risk of suicidal thoughts and behaviors. This slight risk seems to appear during the first four weeks of use and should be monitored very carefully by a person's prescribing doctor.

As a result, the FDA requires that all packaging for antidepressants contain a warning label about the possible risk of suicidal thoughts and behaviors in children and teens. The agency also recommends the close monitoring of children and teens during the first month of treatment for sudden changes in behavior, such as highly active behavior or speech, or for depression symptoms that worsen. These behaviors should be reported to a person's regular doctor or psychiatrist as soon as possible. In general, though, the FDA states that the benefits of using antidepressants for children and teens definitely outweigh the possible risks.

ANTIDEPRESSANTS FOR TREATING OTHER PROBLEMS

Doctors may prescribe antidepressants for disorders besides depression. These include phobias or anxiety disorders, eating disorders, obsessive-compulsive disorder (OCD), attention deficit hyperactivity disorder (ADHD), and significant sleep problems like insomnia.

Severe phobia, panic, or anxiety disorders can interfere with everyday life. Phobias are severe fears about situations or things. For example, you might refuse to leave your house for fear of open or public places, especially those from which escape could be difficult. Some teens might be painfully shy or are always anxious and worried. Panic disorders are conditions in which your fear or anxiety is so strong that it gets in the way of functioning and enjoying life. Panic attacks can be scary. You may have breathing trouble, a racing heartbeat, trembling, dizziness, or a fear of losing control or dying. People who are extremely anxious may also have frequent headaches, upset stomach, or nausea.

The most common teen eating disorders are anorexia nervosa (self-starvation), binge eating (cycles of constantly overeating), and bulimia (overeating and then vomiting). These disorders are fairly common in adolescents, unfortunately, and require medical attention as soon as they are recognized.

Some teens have OCD. Obsessions are constant, reoccurring, and unwanted thoughts or ideas that keep people from thinking about other things. People with obsessions may have extreme fears of harm and may obsess that they will get a deadly disease, for example. Compulsions are urgent, repeated, and irresistible behaviors like washing your hands over and over or checking your schoolwork thirty times for fear that you missed answering a question.

Children or teens with ADHD typically have short attention spans. They have difficulty concentrating or focusing, and they are usually restless. They can often feel frustrated and upset, and they may cause problems in school.

ASK DR. JAN, PSYCHOLOGIST

First name: Wendy

Question:
Lately I don't feel like hanging out with friends, and I'm afraid that if I do go out, people will think I'm always in a bad mood. But if I don't hang out with them, they'll just think I'm not fun. Should I force myself to do things with my friends even if I don't want to?

Answer:
One of the symptoms of depression is lost interest in things you once enjoyed doing. This would include socializing with friends. If we don't do something to address this, the symptoms may just get worse. While it would be a good idea for you to push yourself to engage more with your friends, this may be easier said than done. We all get depressed from time to time. Sadness is a normal emotion. When our feelings of depression become more frequent and intense, it can compromise our functioning at home, in school, with friends, etc. Many studies show that the majority of teenagers who suffer from significant depression do not receive treatment. This is very unfortunate because for most people, depression is a treatable illness. If you find that you cannot get back into socializing like you used to, you may want to meet with a mental health professional to determine if you are experiencing clinical depression and whether counseling would be helpful. While we all know to see our medical doctor when we are having physical symptoms to find out if we need medicine or some other treatment,

we rarely think to do so when we have mental health issues. This is unfortunate because we may not have to suffer needlessly if we get the kind of treatment we need to feel better.

Ask a Question

Do you have a question that you would like answered? E-mail your question to Dr. Jan at drjan@rosenpub.com. If your question is selected, it will appear on the Teen Health & Wellness Web site in "Dr. Jan's Corner."

If you have an urgent question on a health or wellness issue, we strongly encourage you to call a hotline to speak to a qualified professional or speak to a trusted adult, such as a parent, teacher, or guidance counselor. You can find hotlines listed in the For More Information section of this book, or at www. teenhealthandwellness.com/static/hotlines.

BENEFITS OF ANTIDEPRESSANTS

Antidepressants are often an important part of treatment for people of all ages. Teens often receive psychotherapy (talk therapy) along with an antidepressant, since this combined approach usually produces better results. Treatment with antidepressants lifts depression and reduces or eliminates suicidal thinking and behavior. In addition, antidepressants can help teens better communicate about their depression and get the help they need.

Antidepressant medications have been used to treat depression since the 1950s. As scientists have learned more about the way the brain works, they have been able to develop a wide range of antidepressants with minimal side effects. This has been a long process, and it is still being refined. New, more effective, safer drugs are being developed all the time. Antidepressants are not a magic cure, and they are not able to treat all cases of depression. For the majority of people with depression, however, antidepressants can be a safe, effective form of treatment, either alone or in combination with psychotherapy. They do not necessarily make people instantly happy or cause all their problems to go away, but they make the symptoms of depression fade and make life for the depressed person much easier to tackle. There are three major types of antidepressants: tricyclic antidepressants, monoamine oxidase inhibitors (MAOIs), and selective serotonin reuptake inhibitors (SSRIs).

TRICYCLIC ANTIDEPRESSANTS

Tricyclic antidepressants, which include drugs such as Elavil and Norpramin, have been used to treat depression since the late 1950s. They have been shown to be effective for more than 70 percent of people with depression, and until the 1980s, they were the most frequently prescribed type of antidepressant. Tricyclics work by keeping the body from using up too much of its supply of two neurotransmitters: serotonin and norepinephrine. These neurotransmitters have been shown to affect mood.

Unfortunately tricyclic antidepressants have a number of side effects that some patients find difficult to deal with. These side effects include dry mouth, constipation,

Different antidepressants work in different ways. Since all depression is not the same and everyone is different, only a doctor can tell you which course of treatment you should take.

blurred vision, weight gain, rapid heartbeat, dizziness, and drowsiness or sleeplessness, depending on the specific medication prescribed. Tricyclics are related to antihistamines, which are used to treat allergies, and cause some of the same side effects. Patients who use over-the-counter antihistamines for their allergies and take tricyclics may be particularly troubled by side effects. In addition, tricyclics can take as long as two months to have an effect, which can be a problem for people with severe depression or suicidal tendencies. Overdoses of tricyclics, whether intentional or accidental, can be fatal, and this makes them less desirable as a treatment for suicidal patients.

Tricyclics are not usually prescribed for long-term use (more than a year), but they are safe for most people in short-term treatment. They are not recommended for people with a history of heart trouble or high or low blood pressure. Each tricyclic works a little bit differently, so the side effects vary considerably from one medication to another. A psychiatrist may start a patient on one type of tricyclic medication, then switch to a different type if the first one causes too many side effects. Often the psychiatrist can find a tricyclic antidepressant that a patient can take without any side effects just by trial and error. Some tricyclic antidepressants, as well as a related class of drugs called heterocyclic antidepressants, that have been developed recently have fewer side effects than the traditional tricyclics. In the future, these are likely to be prescribed more often than traditional tricyclics.

Monoamine Oxidase Inhibitors (MAOIs)

Monoamine oxidase inhibitors, usually called MAOIs, work by keeping the body from breaking down its supply of three neurotransmitters: dopamine, norepinephrine, and serotonin. They also keep the body from breaking down the amino acid tyramine, which we get from food. An increase of tyramine in the blood supply has been shown to be related to improvements in mood. MAOIs, which have been in use since the late 1950s, are especially effective in treating atypical depression. They are often prescribed if a patient's depression has not responded to other types of antidepressants.

The use of MAOIs must be closely supervised by a psychiatrist because of a potentially dangerous and even fatal side effect. Tyramine increases blood pressure, and because MAOIs increase the supply of tyramine in the blood, they can produce a sudden dramatic increase in blood pressure, which can cause stroke. Patients are at risk for this when they eat foods that contain tyramine. These include cheese (especially aged cheeses), red wine, chocolate, and beans. Some common over-the-counter and prescription medications, such as antihistamines, insulin, and other types of antidepressants, are also dangerous if taken by people who are using MAOIs. If your psychiatrist prescribes an MAOI for you, he or she will give you a list of foods and medications to avoid. You must follow this list carefully because not doing so could be fatal. The rapid increase in blood pressure that an excess of tyramine produces causes a severe, pounding headache, and patients who take MAOIs know that they must seek medical treatment immediately if they develop this type of headache. Some psychiatrists will recommend that patients take a medication to lower blood pressure along with the MAOI.

Other side effects of MAOIs include weight gain, dizziness, and difficulty sleeping. All of these side effects can be controlled, however, and for depressed people who have not had any luck with other types of antidepressants, MAOIs can be a highly effective treatment. The best-known and most widely prescribed MAOIs in the United States are Nardil and Parnate. In Europe, a reversible MAOI has been developed. This new type of MAOI has fewer side effects than the traditional ones and does not require the same dietary changes.

SELECTIVE SEROTONIN REUPTAKE INHIBITORS (SSRIS)

SSRIs are currently the most widely prescribed type of antidepressants. They first became popular in the 1980s. As their name suggests, these drugs work by slowing down the process in which neurons in the brain reabsorb serotonin, one of the neurotransmitters that affects our moods, after one neuron transmits an electrical signal to another. Research has shown that between 60 and 70 percent of people with depression will benefit from the first SSRI that is prescribed for them. Of the patients that are not in this group, some will be helped by a different SSRI. This makes SSRIs among the most effective antidepressants available, and because they have fewer serious side effects than many of the older types of antidepressants, they are widely prescribed.

Prozac is the best known of all the SSRIs, and it is one of the most frequently prescribed drugs of any kind in the United States. When it first became well known as a treatment for depression in the late 1980s, it received a great deal of attention from the media because it helped so many people without the side effects that other antidepressants were known for. Because of its popularity and fame, many people have misconceptions about Prozac. They believe that it will instantly improve a person's mood. There have been reports of people who were not depressed taking Prozac to make them more alert and energetic or to give them an edge. The reality, however, is that Prozac, like other SSRIs, does not begin to have an effect until the patient has been taking it for a period of days or weeks. It is not a mood-altering drug in the usual sense, so it does not produce a high or any other sensation that is immediately noticeable.

Instead, people who take Prozac report that they feel no different when they begin taking the drug, but after a while, they begin to notice that their symptoms of depression are gone. The length of time it takes for symptoms to improve can be as little as two weeks or as long as six weeks or more, depending on the individual and the specific drug. Some patients are frustrated by this waiting period, and they may actually feel worse

Medication alone is usually not sufficient to combat depression. A combination of antidepressants and talk therapy, along with emotional support from family and friends, is often the best path to success.

temporarily or believe that the medication cannot help them. People who have been depressed for a long time may feel elated when their symptoms finally begin to lift—some therapists refer to this as the "Prozac honeymoon"—and that may account for the popular belief that Prozac and other SSRIs will lead to instant happiness.

Another common misconception about Prozac is that it can make people suddenly begin contemplating suicide. When Prozac was still relatively new, there were a handful of reports about patients becoming suicidal while on the drug. Most of the subjects of these reports had had suicidal impulses even before being treated with Prozac,

however, and no scientific study has ever found a direct link between Prozac and thoughts of suicide.

SSRIs do have some minor side effects that vary considerably from person to person. These include headache, feelings of anxiety and restlessness, nausea, and decreased interest in sex. Some people find that a specific SSRI will make them drowsy, whereas another might make them unable to sleep. Most of these side effects are temporary, and switching to a different type of SSRI can eliminate them. Many psychiatrists will start their patients on a low dose of an SSRI in order to avoid even temporary side effects, then gradually increase the dosage as the patient becomes accustomed to the drug. SSRIs can interact with other substances, such as other drugs, which can either increase the effects of those drugs or interfere with them. So it is important to tell your doctor about any medications you are taking before you take an SSRI. SSRIs can also interact with alcohol. Some SSRIs, such as Paxil and Zoloft, seem to have fewer side effects than Prozac. A related class of drugs that affect the body's supply of both serotonin and norepinephrine also have relatively few side effects. These drugs, which include Effexor and Serzone, are increasing in popularity.

Prozac and other SSRIs have generated a great deal of debate in the mental health profession and among the general public. Not all mental health professionals agree with the use of antidepressant medication to treat depression, and the use of medication is a source of some controversy within the psychiatric and psychological professions. Many mental health care providers believe that medication should be used only in conjunction with talk therapy; others believe that antidepressants, especially Prozac and the other SSRIs, are prescribed too frequently or quickly, before the psychiatrist knows the patient well enough to determine whether medication is appropriate.

In addition, some patients—even ones who are chronically depressed, have not had much success with talk therapy alone, and are eager to get help—worry that antidepressants will change their personalities or make them less interesting and creative. This is not literally true, though people who have been depressed for a long time may feel like different people once their symptoms of depression are gone. However, many experts believe that it is essential to treat the biological component of depression with medication. Some even feel that this is more important than treating the emotional aspect with therapy. For most patients, a combination of antidepressants and talk therapy is generally the most effective form of treatment. Just as people with diabetes can control their condition by taking insulin and eating the right kind of foods, people with depression can improve their mental health through a combination of techniques and treatments.

Prozac has been called the "wonder drug," or the "miracle drug," since many people have found that it helps relieve their depression or other problems.

HERBAL MEDICATIONS

In recent years, doctors and patients in the United States have become increasingly interested in natural, plant-based remedies for a variety of illnesses, from arthritis to migraines. Herbal treatments have also been sought for mental disorders. One plant-based remedy in particular, St. John's wort *(Hypericum perforatum)* has been shown to be helpful in treating mild-to-moderate depression. Scientists are not sure exactly how hypericin—the active ingredient in St. John's wort—works, but they know that it does seem to help control depression, sleep disturbances, and tension headaches.

Although it is relatively new in the United States, St. John's wort has been used in Europe for many years. In Germany it is one of the most widely prescribed drugs available. St. John's wort has few serious side effects, although some people may have an allergic reaction to it. Other side effects, which are relatively uncommon, include stomach upset, nausea, increased sensitivity to sunlight, and dizziness. In the United States, the NIMH recently began a study comparing the effectiveness of St. John's wort with that of SSRIs. The NIMH is also studying the long-term safety and usefulness of St. John's wort for people with moderate depression.

The FDA does not consider St. John's wort a drug; instead it is categorized as a dietary supplement. For that reason, it is available without a prescription in drugstores and health food stores. That makes it more affordable and convenient for patients. Unfortunately it also means that it is accessible to anyone who wants to buy it, including people who may not need it or benefit from it. It is dangerous to self-medicate—to take medicine without the advice of a health care professional for any illness, including mental disorders. St. John's wort is generally safe, but it should not be taken with other antidepressants, especially MAOIs. Also, it may not be the most effective treatment for some

Dietary supplements such as St. John's wort are becoming a popular alternative to traditional medication. However, caution should be taken because there is still much to be learned about the effects and side effects of remedies that are not approved by the FDA.

types of depression, and the decision about whether or not to use it should be made by a mental health professional rather than by the patient alone. If your psychotherapist approves of a switch to St. John's wort from a prescription antidepressant, he or she will have you stop taking the prescription medication slowly to wean your body from the drug.

The fact that the FDA does not regulate the sale of dietary supplements also means that there is no way to guarantee the quality of every product labeled as "St. John's wort." As a result, some brands of St. John's wort may not be effective. Products labeled "standardized extract" and containing at least 0.3 percent hypericin are generally reliable,

HERBAL MEDICATIONS (CONTINUED)

but again, it is best to seek advice from a health care professional about the most trustworthy brands.

Another supplement that has recently attracted some interest in the mental health field as well as among the general public is S-adenosylmethionine, better known as SAM-e (pronounced "sammy"). SAM-e is a substance that the human body produces. As a supplement, it is used to treat certain physical disorders such as arthritis, and a number of studies have shown that it is also a helpful treatment for depression. Like St. John's wort, SAM-e is better known in Europe than in the United States. It has minor side effects, including stomach upset, and its long-term safety is not certain. Interest in SAM-e is growing in the United States, and it is likely that it will become more popular and more widely studied in the near future. As with any medication, natural or prescription, SAM-e should not be taken without a health care professional's recommendation.

Although many people have benefited from Prozac, others have not. Some depressed individuals report having violent mood swings or even thoughts of hurting themselves or others while taking Prozac, although it is still not clear if the drug itself or the underlying depression or other disorder is responsible for these feelings. Some say Prozac is prescribed too frequently and under the wrong conditions. This can be very dangerous. It can even make the depression worse by creating other physical and psychological reactions. In other words, Prozac does not work for everyone. Generally speaking, however, when prescribed correctly and in combination with regular checkups with a doctor or therapist, people's positive experiences with Prozac tend to outweigh the negative ones.

Being depressed and taking medication like Prozac does not mean you're "crazy" or that there is something wrong with you any more than taking a medication for diabetes or other health condition does. It means you're recognizing your feelings and doing something positive about your situation. Taking care of yourself is the right choice. But as you would in making any decisions about your health or otherwise, it is important to know all the facts and understand the benefits and risks about taking Prozac. Remember that the best approach is to talk to a trusted source, such as a doctor. There is a lot of information out there, but much of it is inaccurate.

MEDICATIONS FOR BIPOLAR DISORDER

Lithium is a mineral that is commonly found in nature. It is considered a mood stabilizer: it prevents the extremes of mood that are the main characteristic of bipolar disorder. Lithium is the most widely used medication for the treatment of bipolar disorder. Used alone or in combination with sedatives or tranquilizers (which may be prescribed if the patient is violent or is a danger to himself or herself or others), lithium can stop a manic episode and reduce the chance of future episodes occurring.

For some patients, lithium will also lessen the impact of depressive episodes; for others, antidepressants may be prescribed in addition to lithium. Lithium has a number of minor side effects, most of which are temporary.

These may include diarrhea, shaky hands, drowsiness, and weight gain.

The psychiatrist who prescribes lithium will start the patient on a low dose and monitor the level of lithium in the patient's blood. Everyone has a slightly different level of lithium that he or she can tolerate, and the exact dose that is right for a person may change over time. People who take lithium also need to be monitored to make sure that too much of the drug does not build up in their blood over time. More serious (but less common) side effects include changes in thyroid function, which may make a person feel sluggish, exhausted, and cold, and kidney function, which causes thirst and frequent urination. These side effects can be treated with medication, and they are not life threatening. Excessive lithium levels in the blood can cause lithium toxicity, which has symptoms such as confusion, fatigue, blurred vision, rapid or irregular heartbeat, and nausea. It is possible to overdose on lithium, but an overdose can be counteracted and is not necessarily fatal.

Some people with bipolar disorder do not respond to lithium. These patients may be treated with Depakote, a generally safe and effective medication that has some of the same minor side effects as lithium, or Tegretol. Both of these medications control and prevent the rapid mood changes that bipolar disorder causes. A small percentage of people with bipolar disorder will not respond to any of these medications. For these people, antidepressants may help control the depressive episodes, and if the manic episodes are severe, tranquilizers or sedatives may help.

CHAPTER 6

Until the 1980s, psychotherapy of some kind was viewed as the most important and successful way to treat depression. It is still considered important, although there are a growing number of professionals who believe that therapy must be either accompanied by or replaced with treatment with antidepressant medication to succeed. You are probably familiar with the popular image of therapy, in which a patient lying on a couch tells his or her troubles to a bearded, silent man with a German accent. This image stems in part from Sigmund Freud, the Austrian founder of psychoanalysis (which was the first form of psychotherapy) and the person whom many still think of first when they hear the word "psychiatrist." It is a misleading image, however. There are many different forms and theories of psychotherapy, and modern psychotherapy has come a long way from the days of Freud and his couch.

PSYCHOTHERAPY

In simple terms, psychotherapy is treatment for a psychological illness. A psychotherapist may give treatment that includes prescribing medication as well as what is usually referred to as talk therapy—discussing emotional problems and potential solutions with a patient.

While there are many different types of talk therapy, it's almost never a bad idea to open up in general, whether to a doctor, support group, or friends and family.

There are many different types of talk therapy. Some focus on identifying the emotional causes of someone's depression in order to understand and prevent its symptoms, whereas others concentrate more on helping the patient deal with his or her depression and begin feeling better as quickly as possible. Psychotherapy is not a cure for depression; the therapist does not give the patient a magic formula to make the depression go away. Instead, in all forms of psychotherapy, the therapist and the patient work together to try to reduce or eliminate the patient's depression.

THE DIFFERENT TYPES OF THERAPISTS

Therapy can be given by a variety of qualified professionals. These are the ones you are most likely to encounter if you seek treatment for depression:

- Psychiatrists
- Psychologists
- Social workers
- Addiction and substance abuse counselors
- Psychiatric nurses and psychiatric nurse practitioners

In addition, you may be referred to one of these professionals by your family doctor. Each of these specialists has had somewhat different training and education. Training also varies among individuals with the same job title, but the following is a general description of what each type of therapist does. Psychiatrists have graduated from medical school, just as other types of doctors have. In addition, they have been through four years of specialized training in psychiatry. They are the only mental health care providers who can prescribe medications. Many psychiatrists also offer talk therapy for their patients. Others work closely with psychologists or other therapists to plan the best combination of medication and therapy for each patient.

Psychologists have usually completed at least a master's degree, and frequently a doctoral degree, in

Depression is a complex condition, and there are many different types of therapists who treat it. It's good to try several doctors to find the one who's right for you.

psychology. As part of the process of earning a degree, they have done internships in clinics or other mental health centers and have been trained in diagnosing mental disorders. The requirements for becoming a practicing psychologist vary from state to state. Your state's department of health can tell you what the requirements are where you live. Psychologists can provide different types of talk therapy, but they cannot prescribe medication.

Social workers are professionals who have completed a two-year graduate program and earned a master's in social work (MSW). They help people in a variety of ways. Clinical social workers have had specialized training in working with people with emotional problems as well as more general training.

Addiction and substance abuse counselors come from a variety of backgrounds. They may be social workers or psychologists who have had special training in helping people who are recovering from addiction to drugs or alcohol. Some counselors in this field are people who are recovering from addictions themselves. Drug and alcohol abuse are often linked to depression, and therapy with a substance abuse counselor may be recommended for people who are dealing with both.

Psychiatric nurses and nurse practitioners have completed the education and training necessary to become registered nurses, and nurse practitioners have gone through additional training and certification. In addition, these health care professionals have had specialized training in diagnosing and treating mental disorders.

THE DIFFERENT TYPES OF THERAPY

There are many different approaches to talk therapy. Most mental health care professionals have been trained in several of them. If you decide to work with a therapist, you may find that the one you choose favors a particular approach. Others use a combination of approaches to find the best solution for each patient. The types of therapy that are most widely used nowadays include the following.

Cognitive therapy, sometimes called cognitive behavioral therapy, works from the notion that people who are depressed have learned ways of thinking that are negative, inaccurate, and destructive. This type of therapy attempts to change those ways of thinking. Imagine, for example, that you are starting high school in a new city, where you do not know any of your new classmates. A depressed person going into this situation might think, "I'll never make any friends. No one will be interested in being friends with me because everyone will be able to tell what a loser I am." This sort of "automatic thinking" comes easily to people with depression, but it is not an accurate or helpful way of approaching the situation. A cognitive therapist will help the depressed person stop this automatic thinking and instead go into the new school thinking: "This could be a great chance to make some new friends. In such a big school, I know that I will find people who have a lot in common with me."

Cognitive therapy seeks to identify what sort of negative thinking patterns the depressed person has developed, then concentrates on changing those patterns. Most cognitive therapists work with patients for a relatively short period of time. The length of the therapy varies from person to person, but it is generally no more than a few months. The cognitive therapist's aim is to get the depressed patient to feel better and act more positively as quickly as possible.

A recent study by the NIMH suggests that for most people who are mildly to moderately depressed, cognitive therapy is just as effective as, and in some cases more effective than, treatment with antidepressants. Many people find cognitive therapy appealing because it is short-term and is aimed at finding effective solutions.

According to the NIMH study, interpersonal therapy (IPT) is an especially effective treatment for mild or moderate depression and can be helpful for people who are severely depressed as well. This type of therapy focuses on the relationships in a depressed person's life, with the idea that problems in these relationships are the primary cause of the depression. The relationships include those with family members, coworkers, friends, and spouses or partners. The interpersonal therapist works with the depressed patient to find ways to fix problems in relationships and change unrealistic expectations of friends and loved ones that lead to disappointment, frustration, and depression.

Like cognitive therapy, IPT is a relatively short-term form of treatment. Therapy usually lasts for less than six months. It is aimed at ending a depressed person's feelings of isolation and improving the patient's day-to-day functioning in relationships with others.

Psychodynamic psychotherapy is aimed at uncovering problems in a patient's past that are at the root of his or her current depression. In particular, this form of psychotherapy focuses on conflicts and crises in a person's past that were not resolved or were resolved in an unsatisfactory way. Examples of such conflicts include

Psychodynamic psychotherapy aims to address unresolved problems from a person's past, such as enduring tension among family members that can't otherwise be resolved.

an unexpected or early death of a parent, parents' divorce, or difficult relationships with family members that have not been fixed or improved. These unresolved conflicts, according to psychodynamic theory, "haunt" the depressed person and must be studied and understood before the person can move on and enjoy life. One type of psychodynamic therapy, called brief dynamic therapy, focuses only on recent conflicts that are directly related to a current depression. This type of therapy is becoming increasingly popular in treating depression.

Behavioral therapy is similar to cognitive therapy, but instead of focusing on patterns of negative thinking, it looks at negative behavior patterns. The therapist and the patient work together to identify specific behaviors that contribute to the patient's depression, then they find ways to change these behaviors. If, for example, a fear of socializing is making a depressed person feel lonely and unhappy, the therapist may come up with a plan for the patient to spend time with a friend and may offer some sort of reward if the patient does so. The therapist encourages positive behavior in order to break the pattern of negative behavior that is causing or contributing to the patient's problem. Behavioral therapy is often used to treat alcohol and drug addiction as well as phobias and anxiety. It can be helpful in treating depression if the depressed patient is also dealing with substance abuse problems or anxiety disorders.

Psychoanalysis is the oldest form of psychotherapy, started by Freud around the turn of the twentieth century. It seeks to find the causes of emotional problems by studying the patient's past, especially his or her childhood. Using a variety of techniques, the psychoanalyst works to help the patient understand and become more aware of the factors that have shaped his or her emotional state. Psychoanalysis tends to work slowly, often over the course of many years. Because of this, it is not usually the most effective treatment for depression.

ASK DR. JAN, PSYCHOLOGIST

First name: Rakesh

Question:
Sometimes my friends and family ask me what's wrong and I tell them nothing because I don't want them to worry or think I have a problem. But I've heard that talking about your depression helps. What should I do: Tell people about how I feel, or keep it to myself?

Answer:
Usually keeping our feelings to ourselves only serves to make us feel worse. In order to work through negative feelings, they need to be expressed. Whether to a counselor, parent, or friend, it is important that we have people in our lives that we can be genuine and honest with about our feelings. Otherwise our negative feelings get internalized and fuel negative emotions like depression and anger.

Think about why you don't want others to worry or what it would mean if they knew you had a problem. If it is someone who really cares about you, they would want you to tell them the truth. We worry about the people we love and that's a good thing. It's also OK to not be perfect. All of us have problems. Sharing them with those we trust is a sign of strength and not weakness. We all often need help in our lives. There's nothing wrong with being honest about it since that's the best way to really get the help and support that we need.

Ask a Question

Do you have a question that you would like answered? E-mail your question to Dr. Jan at drjan@rosenpub.com. If your question is selected, it will appear on the Teen Health & Wellness Web site in "Dr. Jan's Corner."

If you have an urgent question on a health or wellness issue, we strongly encourage you to call a hotline to speak to a qualified professional or speak to a trusted adult, such as a parent, teacher, or guidance counselor. You can find hotlines listed in the For More Information section of this book, or at www.teenhealthandwellness.com/static/hotlines.

Most depressed people find that short-term therapies aimed at getting them to function and feel better quickly are more effective.

Group therapy allows a group of people to work together, with the help and guidance of a therapist, to find solutions to individual problems. It is not used as often to treat depression as other types of disorders, but it can be helpful for adolescents, who may feel more comfortable discussing problems with their peers rather than one-on-one with an adult.

Family therapy, in which some or all of the members of a family meet together with a therapist to work on problems in family relationships, is not usually used as the primary treatment for depression. Because family issues are often at the root of some types of depression, however, a therapist who is working with a depressed individual may recommend family therapy in addition to one-on-one sessions.

Other types of therapy include alternative approaches such as nutritional therapy, which attempts to improve a person's mental health through dietary changes and the use of herbal remedies such as St. John's wort. Some severe cases of depression, especially psychotic depression, can be successfully treated with electro-convulsive therapy (ECT), sometimes referred to as shock treatment. ECT involves sending electric charges to the brain. Although it was once considered a frightening and even cruel treatment, ECT has been refined over the years so that it is painless and effective. It is usually prescribed when talk therapy and medication have failed to control a patient's depression or if the patient is suicidal or experiences symptoms such as hallucinations and delusions.

MAKING YOUR CHOICE

Many people assume that psychotherapy is expensive and is a luxury that only wealthy people can afford. Although it is true that psychiatrists in private practice often charge high fees (over $100 for a fifty-minute session in some cities), there are many lower-cost options. Psychologists and social workers generally charge somewhat less than psychiatrists do, and mental health clinics are usually more affordable than private practices. In addition, most insurance companies and Medicare plans will pay for at least part of any type of psychotherapy. If your family does not have health insurance, you can find clinics and private individuals who charge a sliding-scale fee, meaning that they will adjust their usual rate according to your family's income. In some cities, free psychotherapy is available at both government-run and privately owned clinics.

With all the different types of therapists available, it can be difficult to decide which is the best choice for you. There are a number of advisers that can help you make your decision. Your primary care provider—the family doctor or nurse practitioner whom you visit each year for a checkup—may be able to suggest an appropriate type of treatment and recommend a specific therapist.

Your family's insurance company, if you have one, may have a system set up for determining the right type of mental health treatment for you. Many health maintenance organizations (HMOs) and managed care companies will require you and your parents to have an intake interview. In this interview, which is often conducted by phone, you will speak to a psychiatric nurse, social worker, or other trained professional about your symptoms and concerns. The interviewer will then recommend a therapist for you to consult and may assist you in setting up an appointment.

Most cities and towns have referral services that you can call or visit. As with an intake interview, a trained staff member will discuss your problems with you and give you the names of three or four therapists who match your needs. You can then contact each of these therapists to find the one who is right for you. Referral services can help you find therapists that specialize in working with adolescents, and they can recommend professionals who accept your family's insurance plan or charge fees based on your or your parents' ability to pay. If your town does not have a referral service, there are national hotlines that you can call for the same sort of assistance.

Your school nurse or guidance counselor most likely has a list of therapists who are specially trained and experienced in working with people your age.

Finding the right therapist is one of the most important steps in the treatment process. The first step is for you and your parents to discuss the idea of going into therapy. In some cases, the decision to see a therapist initially comes from parents. In other cases, the teenager may be the one who first expresses an interest in going into therapy. Either way, you and your parents should be in agreement about the decision if possible. If you are reluctant to see a therapist but your parents insist, you will probably have to go along with their decision as long as you are living under their roof. If this is the case, try to go into your first therapy session with an open mind. If you are reluctant to work with a therapist or refuse to try to do so, your therapy will not be successful in any way.

Before you enter into therapy, you should make sure that you are able to work with the therapist whom you have chosen. You will probably want to speak with a few therapists, usually on the phone, before choosing to make an initial appointment with one. Think about whether you would prefer to talk to a man or a woman, if you have a preference. Make sure that the therapist's office is in a location that you can reach easily and that the therapist has office hours that are convenient for you. The most important question to ask a therapist is whether he or she has experience treating patients with depression. Since teenagers have needs and concerns that are somewhat different from those of adults or younger children, it is best to look for a therapist who regularly works with adolescents.

At your first session, the therapist will ask you how you have been feeling physically and emotionally. He or she will encourage you to talk about what has been troubling you and why you have decided to seek help from a therapist. Most therapists will then tell you about the type of therapy that they think is most appropriate for you and try to give you an estimate of how many sessions you will need. It is not necessary to form a strong opinion about your therapist at the first session, but you should make sure that you feel comfortable talking to her or him. If your therapist makes you uneasy, seems unsympathetic, or is otherwise incompatible, the chances of your therapy being successful are greatly reduced.

If you are seeing a psychiatrist, he or she may discuss antidepressant medication with you and give you a prescription, then refer you to a psychologist or other mental health professional for the talk therapy part of your treatment. A psychologist or clinical social worker, on the other hand, may suggest that you begin a course of medication under the supervision of a psychiatrist or your regular doctor in addition to talk therapy. Medication is not an automatic part of treatment, and it may not be appropriate for you. It is often an important part of successful therapy, however.

THE DECISION TO SEEK HELP

The decision to seek help for a mood disorder can be a difficult one to make. In spite of all that scientists have learned about depression and bipolar disorder in recent years, to some extent our society still regards these conditions as embarrassing and shameful. You may feel that it is a sign of weakness to ask for help, or you may fear being labeled as crazy. Many teens feel that there is no point in talking to anyone—friends, parents, teachers, or other people they trust—because no one will understand

Making the decision to seek help is often a difficult one. It's a good idea to discuss it with friends and family to make sure they're fully aware of the direction you're going.

what they are feeling. On the other hand, it is also possible to think that the symptoms of depression are no big deal, that they are just a normal part of growing up, and that if you just use your willpower, your depression will go away. It is true that any depressive episode will eventually end whether or not it is treated. Without treatment, however, you are likely to experience depressive symptoms again in the future.

Not only is it often difficult to admit that you are depressed, but it may also be hard even to notice. In most cases, depression does not begin overnight. It develops gradually, with symptoms that emerge one by one and slowly get worse over time. This can make it hard for people to recognize that they are depressed. For people with dysthymic disorder, it can be especially difficult because they have felt bad for months and often years, so it may not seem to them that anything about their mood is wrong or out of the ordinary.

All of these concerns are understandable. It is important to remember, though, that struggling with depression does not make you weak, insane, or a bad person. In addition, there are people out there who can help you if you are willing to be helped. It is true that no one person's depression is exactly the same as another person's, but experts now know enough about depression to be able to understand what you are going through and help you find the right treatment. Keep in mind that the majority of people with depression or bipolar disorder can be treated successfully, but they must actively seek treatment.

Perhaps the most important step you will ever take toward feeling better is to ask for help. If you are not willing or able to talk to your parents about getting help for your depression, talk to another adult whom you trust—a teacher, school counselor, therapist at a free clinic, or clergy member. Even a friend may be able to help by talking to concerned adults and helping you find one to confide in. No matter how alone you may feel, there is always someone you can talk to.

OTHER OPTIONS

Some people, particularly those with mild depression or dysthymic disorder, find that after initial treatment with medication and/or talk therapy, they can control their depression and prevent it from recurring on their own through a variety of techniques. Relatively simple ways of taking care of yourself, such as exercising, getting enough sleep, and eating healthily can greatly improve your mood and outlook on life. Studies have shown that exercise can help relieve some symptoms of depression. This is partly because exercise causes the brain to release chemicals called endorphins, which make us feel happy and can lessen physical pain. Exercise is helpful only if you find an activity that you enjoy and stick with it, however. If you have to force yourself to exercise, or if you feel guilty for skipping a workout, the negative effects on your mood may cancel out the positive ones.

Yoga is a form of exercise that many people find helpful both mentally and physically. That is because yoga is "mindful" exercise, requiring you to concentrate on and think carefully about what your body is doing. Meditation and relaxation therapy are also mindful exercises. Consciously relaxing by sitting in a comfortable position, breathing deeply, and focusing on what you are doing at that moment, rather than on your fears and concerns, can be an effective way to fight stress and nervous tension.

Other mindfulness techniques include guided imagery—using your imagination to create and change mental pictures of things that bother you—and biofeedback, which helps you identify and control your mental and physical responses. Both biofeedback and guided imagery are done with the help of a therapist. These are just some of the safe, beneficial techniques that can help you improve your mood, physical health, and the way you look at life. They are not substitutes for psychotherapy, but they can be used at the

While there are many types of treatment for depression, sometimes the best ones are the simplest. Relaxation techniques such as yoga can help relieve symptoms of depression.

same time as therapy and continued once your therapy has stopped. If any of these approaches interests you, discuss it with your therapist, who will either tell you more about it or help you find someone who can.

PREVENTING SUICIDE

When someone says the word "suicide," it is usually met with silence. Just say the word, and immediately people want to avoid talking about the subject. Suicide describes the voluntary and intentional act of taking one's own life. It comes from two Latin root words, *sui* (of oneself) and *cidium* (a killing or slaying). It is very difficult to understand an act that is contrary to living one's day-to-day life. Most people want to experience aging, not to end their life prematurely.

Unfortunately people are not transparent; you cannot look into their heads to see what they are thinking or feeling. Most people go through their day looking at people but not really seeing individuals. They might not notice that what they are seeing could be the person's cry for help. Is it the person who comes from the perfect family but feels that he or she does not measure up? Or is it someone who comes from an abusive family? Do you connect with the person who is always eating alone, an isolate? Do you see the person begging for help but not voicing it? Seeing people and connecting with them could be the first step in suicide prevention.

If you are a teenager contemplating suicide, you may want to talk openly about your thoughts, but you may think society seems unwilling to hear them. You may start to feel isolation and emotional pain and may begin to feel more and more alone. If you could have the opportunity to talk openly about your feelings, you may finally feel understood. By not keeping suicide under lock and key and trying to understand its occurrence, there could possibly be a means of preventing it from happening to you or someone you know.

Taking one's life has occurred throughout history. Even today, news stories tell of people taking their own lives. Young suicide bombers give up their lives for what they see as noble causes. Suicide continues to be a major concern in today's society, and the problem is not lessening or going away.

You probably have heard of or know friends, family members, famous stars, or acquaintances who have ended their lives through the act of suicide. Suicide is the eighth leading cause of death in the United States. It is estimated that five million people now living in the United States have attempted suicide. The World Health Organization (WHO) estimates that the suicide rate worldwide could rise to 1.5 million suicides per year by the year 2020. Dr. Catherine Le Galès-Camus of WHO says, "Suicide is a tragic global public health problem. Worldwide, more people die from suicide than from all homicides and wars combined."

It is very frightening when you look at suicide statistics for young men and women. Look at the face of a clock and start counting. Approximately once every eighty seconds, a teenager attempts to take his or her own life; about once every one hundred minutes, a teen actually completes a suicide. After car accidents and murder, suicide is the third leading cause of death for fifteen- to twenty-four-year-olds in the United States.

Suicide rates among ten- to fourteen-year-olds have nearly doubled in the past few decades. White teenage boys have the highest rate of suicide. Black teenagers are now more than twice as likely to kill themselves as they were twenty years ago. Out of every five people who take their own lives, four are likely to be male. Females are three times more likely to attempt suicide, but males are the ones who complete their attempts. Males tend to use more violent methods, like shooting themselves, than women do. Women might use pills; therefore, some can be saved. Recently, many teenage girls who have died by suicide have used violent methods like guns. Gun deaths continue to be on a steady climb. Frighteningly, nearly 60 percent of all suicides in the United States are completed with a gun.

The suicide rate for teen girls has skyrocketed recently, shocking and puzzling experts. Suicide rates among fifteen- to nineteen-year-old girls rose 32 percent between 2003 and 2004, based on the most recent data available in 2007. Rates for males in that age group rose, too—but only by 9 percent. And the suicide rate for preteen and young teen girls, aged ten to fourteen, jumped a staggering 76 percent. Experts are scrambling for answers and asking themselves: why has this happened?

The rate of suicide for teens may even be higher than reported. Automobile crashes account for the leading cause of death for fifteen- to nineteen-year-olds. Law enforcement officials might look at a car crash of a single teenage driver, see no skid marks, and put down the cause as "accident." In fact, these car crashes could be "autocides," the term for suicide by car crash.

The suicide rate among U.S. teens remained high for a second consecutive year in 2005 (the most recent year for which data is available as of 2008), according to a study. Experts suggest that the fear of antidepressants—and their possible side effect of causing suicidal thoughts—may have curtailed use of the drugs. They say that fear of these drugs may ironically lead more teens to suffer from severe depression and commit suicide.

The transition into adulthood can be difficult. As an adolescent, you are part of a particularly vulnerable group that can encounter pressure from your family and peer groups. Some problems you may face include family breakdown; sexuality; body imagery (anorexia, bulimia, obesity); and social, school, and peer pressures. These problems could lead to a state of depression, which is the most common cause of suicide.

Teens already have a difficult time coping with the demands of school, family, and friends—but what if you add poverty into the mix? The pressure is too much for some teens, and a joint study by Canada's Université de Montréal and Tufts University concluded that teens from poorer communities are four times as likely to commit suicide than their peers from wealthier neighborhoods.

HELPING FRIENDS AND FAMILY

Having a friend who is dealing with depression can be very stressful. You may be afraid that you will give him or her bad advice or that you will let your friend down if you are not able to help. You may even have heard that talking about depression makes it worse; this is not true, although some people believe that it is. If you are dealing with problems of your own, you may find it too hard to take on someone else's problems, too. You may feel burdened by your friend's troubles or even begin to resent him or her for asking you to help instead of working things out for himself or herself. You may feel neglected or hurt if your friend doesn't think that your help is enough. In fact, you cannot solve your friend's problems if he or she is clinically depressed any more than you would be able to cure a friend's cold or heal his or her broken leg. There are, however, some things that friends can do for friends who are suffering from mood disorders:

- Know the symptoms of depression and bipolar disorder so that you can help friends find help if their symptoms are serious and are not just a temporary case of the blues.
- Let friends know that you will support them no matter how depressed they are. Be a good listener; do not judge your depressed friends or make fun of their feelings.
- Be aware of signs that someone is considering suicide. If a friend begins to show any of these signs, talk to a trusted adult immediately. There is a common myth that people who talk about suicide do not really intend to go through with it. This is not true; talking about suicide is often an early sign that someone is planning to kill himself or herself.
- Be prepared to talk to a concerned adult about your friend's problems if the friend refuses to get help on his or her own, even if doing so means that your friend may be angry with you or feel betrayed. Usually this anger will be only temporary, and your

friend will eventually come to appreciate what you have done. Even if your friend never forgives you, it is better to have helped him or her get treatment for depression than to stay friends and risk having the depression worsen.

- Do not assume that your friend's problems will take care of themselves or that you can make the problems go away.

Being a teenager is hard for almost everyone, and being a depressed teenager is even harder. But no matter how depressed you are, help is out there. There is no reason to feel shame or guilt if you are depressed. Depression is an illness like any other—even though it is also unique—and the best thing you can do for depression, as for any illness, is to seek treatment. It will not be easy, and you won't find a magical cure. Therapy takes work and can itself be painful and difficult, although only temporarily. But it will help, and you will feel better. The sooner you look for help, the sooner your life will begin to improve. It takes strength and courage to ask for help, but it is even harder to battle depression on your own. Don't suffer any longer than you have to—and remember, you are not alone.

Monoamine oxidase inhibitors (MAOIs)

Generic Name	Brand Name
Isocarboxazid	Marplan
Moclobemide	Aurorix, Manerix
Phenelzine	Nardil
Selegiline	Eldepryl, Zelapar, Emsam
Tranylcypromine	Parnate

Norepinephrine-dopamine releasing agents (NDRAs)

Generic Name	Brand Name
Amphetamine	Adderall
Dextroamphetamine	Dexedrin
Dextromethamphetamine	Desoxyn
Lisdexamfetamine	Vyvanse
Tricyclic antidepressant	TCAs
Amitriptyline	Elavil, Ende
Clomipramine	Anafranil
Desipramine	Norpramin, Pertofrane
Dosulepin	Dothiepin, Prothiaden

Doxepin	Adapin, Sinequan
Imipramine	Tofranil
Lofepramine	Feprapax, Gamanil, Lomont
Nortriptyline	Pamelor
Protriptyline	Vivactil
Trimipramine	Surmontil

Norepinephrine reuptake inhibitors (NRIs)

GENERIC NAME	BRAND NAME
Viloxazine	Vivalan

Norepinephrine-dopamine reuptake inhibitors (NDRIs)

GENERIC NAME	BRAND NAME
Dexmethylphenidate	Focalin
Methylphenidate	Ritalin, Concerta

Selective serotonin reuptake inhibitors (SSRIs)

GENERIC NAME	BRAND NAME
Citalopram	Celexa
Escitalopram	Lexapro, Cipralex
Paroxetine	Paxil, Seroxat
Fluoxetine	Prozac

| Fluvoxamine | Luvox |
| Sertraline | Zoloft, Lustral |

Serotonin-norepinephrine reuptake inhibitors (SNRIs)

GENERIC NAME	BRAND NAME
Desvenlafaxine	Pristiq
Duloxetine	Cymbalta
Milnacipran	Ixel, Savella
Venlafaxine	Effexor

Tetracyclic antidepressants (TeCAs)

GENERIC NAME	BRAND NAME
Amoxapine	Asendin
Maprotiline	Ludiomil
Mianserin	Bolvidon, Norval, Tolvon

Others

GENERIC NAME	BRAND NAME
Buspirone	Buspar
Trazodone	Desyrel
Reboxetine	Edronax, Vestra
Mirtazapine	Remeron
Nefazodone	Serzone
Bupropion	Wellbutrin

ABOUT DR. JAN

Dr. Jan Hittelman is a licensed psychologist with over twenty years of experience working with teens, children, adults, and families in a variety of settings.

In addition to clinical practices in California, Colorado, and New York, he has specialized in program development in partnership with school systems, psychiatric hospitals, correctional facilities and the courts, outpatient settings, residential treatment facilities, and private nonprofit organizations.

He founded Compass House, a nonprofit counseling collaborative for teens and their families. He launched Boulder Psychological Services in 2007.

Dr. Hittelman also authors a monthly newspaper column entitled "Surviving the Teenage Years" in the *Boulder Daily Camera*, writes monthly columns for the Boulder Valley School District under the sponsorship of the Parent Engagement Network, and publishes an online question-and-answer column for teens in the Rosen Publishing Group's online resource Teen Health & Wellness.

Teen Health & Wellness: Real Life, Real Answers (*http://www.teenhealthandwellness.com*) is a database designed for teens on issues relating to health, fitness, alcohol, drugs, mental health, family life, and much more. Check your school or local library for access.

GLOSSARY

antidepressant A drug prescribed by a doctor to treat depression.

anxiety An extreme state of nervousness or fear.

bipolar disorder A mental disorder whose sufferers experience extreme swings of depression and elation.

compulsion An uncontrollable urge to do something.

depression A mental illness in which sadness overwhelms a person's life.

diagnosis The identification of an illness following an examination.

disorder A psychological abnormality usually caused by a disease or abnormal environmental condition.

dopamine A chemical in the brain that acts as a neurotransmitter and is involved in the formation of epinephrine.

dual diagnosis A condition in which a person suffers from both a mental illness and a substance abuse problem.

gene A unit of heredity that is transferred from a parent to offspring and is held to determine some characteristic of the offspring.

mania A state of unnatural excitement or enthusiasm.

MAOI (monoamine oxidase inhibitor) An antidepressant that suppresses the production of monoamine oxidase in the brain and so allows monoamines to accumulate.

neurotransmitter A chemical that is transmitted across the synapse or junction and transfers impulses to another structure.

obsession A strong fixation on an idea.

phobia A focused and extreme fear of a particular state of being.

Prozac The trade name for the SSRI antidepressant that boosts the activity of serotonin in the brain.

psychotherapy Also known as talk therapy, a process in which a person tries to heal depression by talking to a therapist about his or her feelings and experiences.

serotonin A chemical that acts as a neurotransmitter.

side effect An indirect effect of a drug or medical treatment.

SSRI Selective serotonin reuptake inhibitor, a drug that increases the activity of serotonin in the brain.

suicide The intentional killing of one's self.

therapist A person trained to help patients recover from mental or physical illness or cope with daily life.

thyroid A gland that regulates development through the rate of metabolism.

tricyclic On the molecular level, a class of antidepressant drugs having molecules with three fused rings.

FOR MORE INFORMATION

American Psychiatric Association
1000 Wilson Boulevard, Suite 1825
Arlington, VA 22209-3901
(703) 907-7300
Web site: http://www.psych.org

Founded in 1844, the American Psychiatric Association is the world's largest psychiatric organization representing more than thirty-eight thousand psychiatric physicians from around the world.

American Psychological Association
750 1st Street NE
Washington, DC 20002-4242
(202) 336-5510
Web site: http://www.apa.org

The American Psychological Association is the largest association of psychologists worldwide with 150,000 members. Its mission is "to advance the creation, communication and application of psychological knowledge to benefit society and improve people's lives."

Depression and Bipolar Support Alliance (DBSA)
730 N. Franklin Street, Suite 501
Chicago, IL 60654-7225
(800) 826-3632
Web site: http://www.dbsalliance.org

Founded in 1985, the alliance is the "leading patient-directed national organization focusing on the most prevalent mental illnesses," according to its Web site.

iFred

P.O. Box 17598

Baltimore, MD 21297-1598

(800) 789-2647

Web site: http://www.ifred.org

IFred is a nonprofit organization dedicated to "Bringing Depression Hope." The organization helps research the causes of depression and support those affected by the condition.

MedlinePlus

Depression

National Library of Medicine

8600 Rockville Pike

Bethesda, MD 20894

(888) FIND-NLM [346-3656]

Web site: http://www.nlm.nih.gov/medlineplus/depres-
   sion.html

MedlinePlus is a division of the National Institutes of Health that offers medical advice to patients and their families and friends.

Mental Health America

2000 N. Beauregard Street, 6th Floor

Alexandria, VA 22311

(800) 969-6642

Web site: http://www.nmha.org

This is the nation's largest and oldest community-based network dedicated to helping all Americans live mentally healthier lives.

National Alliance for Research on Schizophrenia and Depression (NARSAD)
60 Cutter Mill Road, Suite 404
Great Neck, NY 11021
(800) 829-8289
Web site: http://www.narsad.org
Founded in 1987, the NARSAD helps fund mental health research by raising money from donors from around the world.

National Institute of Mental Health (NIMH)
Science Writing, Press, and Dissemination Branch
6001 Executive Boulevard, Room 8184, MSC 9663
Bethesda, MD 20892-9663
(866) 615-6464
Web site: Web site: http://www.nimh.nih.gov
The NIMH envisions a world in which mental illnesses are prevented and cured.

WEB SITES

Due to the changing nature of Internet links, Rosen Publishing has developed an online list of Web sites related to the subject of this book. This site is updated regularly. Please use this link to access the list:

http://www.rosenlinks.com/411/dep

FOR FURTHER READING

Biegel, Gina M. *The Stress Reduction Workbook for Teens: Mindfulness Skills to Help You Deal with Stress* (Instant Help). Oakland, CA: New Harbinger Publications, 2010.

Cobain, Bev, and Elizabeth Verdick. *When Nothing Matters Anymore: a Survival Guide for Depressed Teens*. Minneapolis, MN: Free Spirit Pub., 2007.

Griffith, Gail. *Will's Choice: A Suicidal Teen, a Desperate Mother, and a Chronicle of Recovery*. New York, NY: HarperCollins, 2006.

Gunaratana, Bhante Henepola. *Beyond Mindfulness in Plain English: An Introductory Guide to Deeper States of Meditation*. Somerville, MA: Wisdom Publications, 2009.

Knaus, William. *The Cognitive Behavioral Workbook for Anxiety: A Step-by-Step Program*. Oakland, CA: New Harbinger Publications, 2008.

Knaus, William. *The Cognitive Behavioral Workbook for Depression: A Step-by-Step Program*. Oakland, CA: New Harbinger Publications, 2006.

Kornfield, Jack. *Meditation for Beginners*. Louisville, CO: Sounds True, 2008.

Levin, Judith. *Depression and Mood Disorders* (Teen Mental Health). New York, NY: Rosen Publishing Group, 2008.

Liebler, Nancy, and Sandra Moss. *Healing Depression the Mind-Body Way: Creating Happiness with*

Meditation, Yoga, and Ayurveda. Hoboken, NJ: Wiley, 2009.

Luciani, Joseph J. *Self-Coaching: The Powerful Program to Beat Anxiety and Depression.* 2nd ed. Hoboken, NJ: Wiley, 2006.

Miller, Allen R., Ph.D. *Living with Depression* (Teen's Guides). New York, NY: Checkmark Books, 2008.

O'Connor, Richard. *Undoing Depression: What Therapy Doesn't Teach You and Medication Can't Give You.* New York, NY: Little, Brown and Company, 2010.

Schab, Lisa M. *The Anxiety Workbook for Teens: Activities to Help You Deal with Anxiety & Worry.* Oakland, CA: New Harbinger Publications, 2008.

Schab, Lisa M. *Beyond the Blues: A Workbook to Help Teens Overcome Depression.* Oakland, CA: Instant Help Books, 2008.

Schachter, Michael B., and Deborah R. Mitchell. *What Your Doctor May Not Tell You About Depression: The Breakthrough Integrative Approach for Effective Treatment.* New York, NY: Wellness Central, 2006.

Strosahl, Kirk, and Patricia J. Robinson. *The Mindfulness & Acceptance Workbook for Depression: Using Acceptance & Commitment Therapy to Move Through Depression & Create a Life Worth Living.* Oakland, CA: New Harbinger Publications, 2008.

Van Dijk, Sheri, and Karma Guindon. *The Bipolar Workbook for Teens: DBT Skills to Help You Control Mood Swings.* Oakland, CA: Instant Help Books, 2010.

Williams, Mark, et al. *The Mindful Way Through Depression: Freeing Yourself from Chronic Unhappiness.* New York: The Guilford Press, 2007.

Zucker, Faye, and Joan E. Huebl. *Beating Depression: Teens Find Light at the End of the Tunnel.* New York, NY: Children's Press, 2007.

INDEX

ABOUT THE AUTHORS

Michael Owens is a writer living in New Jersey, and Amy Gelman is a writer living in New York City.

PHOTO CREDITS